THE FAT BLOCKER DIET

Other Books by Arnold Fox, M.D.

The Beverly Hills Medical Diet
DLPA to End Chronic Pain and Depression
Wake Up! You're Alive
Immune for Life
Making Miracles
Beyond Positive Thinking
The Healthy Prostate
Alternative Healing
Natural Relief from Pain and Depression

Other Books by Brenda Adderly, M.H.A.

The Complete Guide to Pills
The Arthritis Cure

THE
FAT BLOCKER
DIET

THE REVOLUTIONARY DISCOVERY
THAT REMOVES FAT NATURALLY

✦

ARNOLD FOX, M.D.,
and
BRENDA ADDERLY, M.H.A.

Foreword by Elizabeth Muss, M.D., F.A.C.C.

St. Martin's Press ✹ New York

Design by Stanley S. Drate/Folio Graphics Co. Inc.

Another book by Affinity Communications Corp.

ISBN: 0-312-17102-1

First Edition: May 1997

10 9 8 7 6 5 4 3 2 1

To all of my patients, past, present, and future,
who trusted and taught me.
—ARNOLD FOX, M.D.

✦

And to the countless numbers who love food but are tired of
struggling against it.
—BRENDA ADDERLY, M.H.A.

Contents

Acknowledgments

Since this book is a cooperative effort, to which we each brought our own knowledge and experience, we would like to thank together the many people who helped us create it, and individually those who have helped us personally and prepared us for this work.

Together, above all, we would like to thank Barry Fox, Arnold Fox's son (and Brenda Adderly's collaborator on both a prior and a future book), who played a major role in crafting this book. Barry is a fine writer, a sweet man, a good friend, and a wonderful son.

We would also like to thank Jeremy Katz, our brilliant and determined editor at St. Martin's Press, for his confidence in us and in this book. And we would also like to express our deepest appreciation to: Elizabeth Carol Muss, M.D., F.A.C.C., who (aside from writing our foreword) reviewed the entire manuscript with care; Nadine Taylor, M.S.R.D., for reviewing the nutritional aspects of the book; and Dr. Fox's wife, Hannah, for carefully reviewing the manuscript and correcting our mistakes.

Arnold Fox would like to thank WellQuest of New York, New York, for providing him with early information on Chitosan, as well as Chitosan Plus for use in his testing. And, importantly, he would like to thank his patients.

He would also like to thank Howard Cohl of Affinity Communications for listening to his stories about South Philly. Dr. Fox also emphasizes his deep gratitude to those of his teachers and colleagues whose knowledge he used in the preparation of this book: Earl Mindell, Ph.D.; Hans Selye, M.D.; Richard Weiner, Ph.D.; C. Norman Shealy, M.D., D.Sc.; and Linus Pauling, Ph.D. He offers a special thanks to Jim McGuire, Esq., for providing voluminous quantities of information on Chitosan.

Finally, to his 4-year-old granddaughter, Heather, who sat in his lap while he wrote the book, he says, "I dearly love you, and thanks for being you."

Brenda Adderly would like to thank Peter Engel of Affinity Communications for his commitment to disseminating important medical information to the public. Also, she would like to thank both Paul J. Rosch, M.D., F.A.C.P., and Edward R. Downe, Jr., for enlightening her about the miracle of Chitosan.

Foreword

My credo is that it's never too early to learn how to care for your heart. In my cardiology practice I emphasize the importance of patient education—an educated patient is a healthy patient. The more my patients understand about what keeps their hearts and bodies working properly, the longer they will live. Moreover, they will do so with a better quality of life. Heart disease may get us in the end, but with appropriate care it can be delayed for decades, leaving us with years and years of good, healthy, productive living.

High cholesterol is a leading contributor to heart disease. The optimum serum cholesterol level is 150, but the majority of Americans have levels well above this. That is a significant health risk. Maintaining a 150 cholesterol level often requires more intervention than just modest diet modification. Rather, it usually calls for either a severely restricted diet, which is hard for most people to stick to, or the use of powerful drugs with possibly undesirable side effects.

However, before I implement either of these rather draconian approaches, I recommend that my patients try Chitosan, the Fat Blocker. It effectively lowers the level of low-density lipoprotein (LDL, or the "bad" cholesterol that comes from saturated fat) without any known harmful side effects. It is a natural, safe option that I wholeheartedly endorse. In fact, I have been using the Fat Blocker to lower cholesterol and promote weight control in my patients since 1995.

The Fat Blocker, as you will learn in this book, is a super fiber that binds up the saturated fat from the foods we eat before it has a chance to be absorbed into the body. Instead of the fat entering the bloodstream and causing an increase in both LDL and weight, it simply attaches itself to the Chitosan and is carried harmlessly through the body.

One of the positive side benefits of this fat binding effect is weight loss. Excessive weight is a major contributor to many diseases and conditions in addition to heart disease (cancer, diabetes, and gallstones). Therefore, maintaining an appropriate weight level should be one of the top priorities in maintaining good health.

Unfortunately, as we all know, diets are hard to adhere to, which probably accounts for the fact that there seems to be a new diet fad around every corner. The Fat Blocker, while little known up to now, is a powerful and easy weight-loss tool. If patients keep with their daily routine without making any changes other than adding the Fat Blocker, they are almost bound to reduce the fat from their food intake. Less fat means less calories; less calories means less weight.

The Fat Blocker works beautifully. My patients report losing weight without the hardship of rigorous diet regimens or excessive exercise. They can have an occasional splurge (which I firmly believe in) and not upset their diet. They can still enjoy their lives—and lose weight. I'm enthusiastic about the Fat Blocker. Here is a way my patients can improve their health in a safe, natural, relatively easy way.

The fact is, you *will* lose weight with the Fat Blocker, provided that you maintain sound health, eat sensibly, and exercise regularly. You do not have to do these things to extremes. With reasonable behavior, not only will you benefit physically, but your mental health will receive an ongoing boost.

The Fat Blocker can lower your cholesterol level, cause you to lose weight, and contribute significantly to your overall health.

I'd like to compliment Dr. Fox and Brenda Adderly on *The Fat Blocker Diet*. The recommendations in this book with respect to Chitosan and modifications to one's diet represent the advice I've given over the years. It is a balanced approach that emphasizes a judicious use of supplements *without* replacing food.

—ELIZABETH CAROL MUSS, M.D., F.A.C.C.

Dr. Muss has practiced cardiology for over 20 years in New York City. She is one of only seven female cardiologists in private practice. A graduate of New York Medical College, Dr. Muss is an Assistant Clinical Professor of Medicine at Cornell University Medical College. She is an Associate Attending Physician at New York Hospital, an Associate Attending Physician at Beth Israel Medical Center, and sits on the Medical Board of Beth Israel. Dr. Muss earned her Diplomate in Cardiovascular Disease in 1977, and is a member of the American Woman's Medical Association and the New York Cardiology Association.

A Note on Style

This book is truly a joint effort. Many sentences were started by one of us and completed by the other. And we each contributed to the book our separately acquired knowledge about Chitosan. Dr. Fox's contribution came from his vast experience as a practicing physician, an internist, and cardiologist who has helped many thousands of patients to lose weight and from his own observations in prescribing Chitosan. Brenda Adderly's contribution comes from her experience and know-how as a researcher and "health care detective."

However, while this book was a fully collaborative effort, we found it disruptive to the flow of the writing to have to identify from which of our experience a particular anecdote or example was drawn. Therefore, since many of the case histories cited did come from Dr. Fox's practice, we have chosen to write the whole book in his voice. We wish the reader to be clear, however, that every view expressed is jointly held, and that every recommendation is jointly supported.

The Fat Blocker Philosophy

Everyone who takes Chitosan will benefit from having less fat in their blood and body cells. But those who couple Chitosan with the low-fat diet and exercise program I describe in this book will benefit the most.

Chitosan is an important part of my Fat Blocker Program, but remember

+ Chitosan is not meant to replace healthful eating habits. You should be following a low-fat diet as a matter of course.

+ Do not use Chitosan as an excuse to binge. The correct use of Chitosan is as an adjunct to a healthful diet—a way to assist you in achieving your goals.

+ Although some people will lose weight by taking Chitosan alone, I find that almost everyone does better when they couple the supplement with the sensible, easy-to-follow low-fat, high-fiber diet I describe in this book.

+ Remember that Chitosan only blocks *fat*. Most of the high-calorie goodies we enjoy, including candy, cake, pastries, and pies, also contain large amounts of sugar, which is not blocked by the Chitosan. So, if you're not careful, you can end up gaining weight even though you've effectively blocked the absorption of fat.

A Note to Readers

Caution: Do not use Chitosan if you are allergic to shellfish, are pregnant or lactating, or are under the age of 14. Although we are not aware of any evidence that Chitosan can be dangerous for these groups, it's best to be safe.

The material in this book is for information purposes only. It is not intended to be a prescription for you, or to replace the advice of your physician. Please discuss all aspects of this or any other program with your medical doctor *before* beginning. If you have any medical conditions, or are taking any prescription or nonprescription medications, see your physician before beginning a program, or altering or discontinuing the use of any of your medications.

Since Chitosan blocks fat, it is theoretically possible that it might block a portion of fat-soluble vitamins, including A, D, and E. Therefore, I advise my patients to take their vitamins with the morning meal and/or late at night, when no Chitosan is taken.

THE FAT BLOCKER DIET

1

◆

Why Can't I Lose Weight?

Claire, a 48-year-old, 200-pound nurse whom I've known for many years, recently showed me her computerized "diet database."

"Look at this, Dr. Fox," she said proudly, pointing to the computer screen. "Here's a list of the diets I've been on, arranged alphabetically." It looked like there were 30 or 40 diets on the screen, from Atkins down to Zone.

New words and numbers appeared on the screen moments after she tapped a few keys on the keyboard. "Now they're arranged by pounds lost. See?" She pointed to the first item on the list. "I lost 50 pounds on liquid protein, that's the most, then 42 pounds when my jaw was wired and 28 pounds on this fruit-only diet. And look at this."

The display changed as she tapped a few more keys. "Now I've got them listed by amounts of weight regained after going off the diet. And the list in this column shows the side effects of each diet." She sat back in her chair, smiling proudly. "This is the most complete record of dieting ever compiled. By name, by dates that I was on the diet, by pounds lost, pounds gained, side effects, and cost; I've got it all." Her smile faded as she continued. "Unfortunately, I've also still got all the fat I started with."

* * *

Claire is not alone. One out of every three American adults is obese[1] and millions more are carrying around too much fat and becoming obese. Despite the fitness craze that arose in the 1970s and still continues, America is *not* a slim and healthy nation. But we certainly *want* to be (and quickly), so we turn to fad diets.

In the early years of my practice of internal medicine and cardiology, I put many people on weight-loss diets in an attempt to improve their health. But things did not go nearly as well as I had hoped. In fact, I once joked to a colleague, "I think I'm running a weight *gain* practice." Many of my patients were actually getting heavier on the unimpressive diets we doctors used to recommend back in the 1950s and 1960s.

In the 40 years I've practiced medicine, I've seen every kind of diet you can imagine: water diets, grapefruit diets, the Drinking Man's Diet, the Stillman and Atkins diets, pineapple diets, starvation diets, no-carbohydrate diets, starch-blocking diets, diets with pills, diets without pills, "scientific" diets, "common sense" diets, army diets, air force diets, American diets, foreign diets, liquid diets, and liquid-protein diets. I learned about these diets from my colleagues, from the medical literature, from my patients, from my secretary, from my wife, even from *Reader's Digest* and *The Ladies' Home Journal*.

Obesity Versus Overweight

Obesity and overweight are not the same thing. To be overweight simply means to weigh more than standard or average for your height and body type. Many professional football players are overweight. However, their excess pounds are usually made of muscle, so they're not obese. The term "obesity," on the other hand, refers to excess fat, which is always dangerous. A person doesn't have to weigh too much to be obese—I've known models who qualify.

My patients have always asked me which diet was the best, which one they should be on. I knew you could lose a lot of weight quickly on almost any of the diets, but I always hesitated to recommend one. Once I was approached by a manufacturer of the supplement used in the Starch-Blocker Diet, who asked me to say something positive about the pill. As I spoke with the manufacturer, I realized that he didn't know how much trouble this starch-blocking supplement could create as it blocked the ability of the pancreas to make an enzyme called amylase. Sure enough, many people who went on this diet suffered from nausea, vomiting, and other problems. The moral of the story is you must learn everything you can about a diet or supplement before you take it, and avoid it if the answers are not positive.

The problem with most all the fad diets is they are ill conceived, ineffective in the long run, and often dangerous. The originators and purveyors of these diets do

It's Not Fair!

Many people do manage to stay thin. Some of them do it by sheer will power, eating sparingly and exercising vigorously. Others seem to eat whatever they want, laze around, but never put on any weight. How do they do it?

Clearly, there are genetically inherited differences in the way we metabolize calories. Some of us are simply destined to be slimmer than others.

Scientists specializing in obesity believe that, up to the age of about two, our bodies generate an increasing number of fat cells. The number produced depends on how much we are fed. After that, we neither increase or reduce the number of those cells in our bodies. Instead, our existing fat cells either expand or contract depending on our eating and exercise habits. People who did not develop an excess of fat cells when they were babies and children will have a lessened tendency to grow fat later in life, and will find it easier to lose weight if they do.

not understand (or have chosen to ignore) the underlying meaning and rationale of diets. Most of us think of a diet as a quick way to lose weight. We see it as a temporary device, a way to control ourselves or juggle food around. And once we've lost the desired amount of weight, we quickly and happily discard it.

The word "diet" comes from the Greek word "diaita," which means a mode of life or a regimen. A diet, then, is not a temporary aid to be dropped and forgotten when the weight-loss goal is met. Instead, it is a lifelong plan, a blueprint for your life and health.

Where Does Fat Come From?

Carbohydrates, whether they enter your mouth in the form of simple or complex carbohydrates, are eventually broken down into glucose. The glucose is then used for energy or stored in the muscle cells and liver for future use. This stored glucose is called glycogen. Excess glucose is also driven into the fat cells and stored as tryiglycerides (fat).

Fat cells are called adipocytes (ad-i-po-sites). A typical adipocyte looks like a large circle with a small circle sticking out of it. The small circle is the cell nucleus, pushed to the side by the fat that fills the adipocyte. Adipocytes are specifically designed to "grab" fat by binding with the lipoproteins that carry fat through the bloodstream.

About half of the total fat in the body is stored in fat cells just under the skin (subcutaneous). Most of the remaining fat is packed around the organs in your abdominal cavity (such as the heart, kidneys, etc.).

Overeating leads to the accumulation of excess calories, which is, of course, stored as fat. To make room for the new fat, your fat cells must expand, because you can't manufacture new fat cells once you've passed adolescence. Unfortunately, fat cells are pretty pliable—it seems there's always room for them to grow.

You can lose weight (at least temporarily) on just about any diet. But before you do, ask yourself 2 very important questions:

How are you losing the weight? And how will the process affect your health?

There are three ways to lose weight: 1) By getting rid of water in your tissues; 2) By forcing your body to consume lean body tissue such as the heart, lungs, kidneys, or muscles; or 3) By burning fatty tissue.

Losing water weight, as you do with the high-protein diets and diuretics, is absolutely worthless because you will quickly replace the lost water and find yourself right back where you started. Losing and regaining water is not only a big waste of time and money, but it can also cause you to lose vital minerals, which can prompt serious medical problems.

Cutting into your lean body tissue is also a dangerous, possibly deadly, approach. Vital organs can become undermined, leading to organ damage and even organ failure. The only safe, sound, and permanent weight-loss method is burning off excess fat. Doing so takes time and patience, but fad diet promoters would rather promise quick and easy weight loss. Unfortunately, their promises are usually just hot air. Numerous studies have shown that 95 percent of those who lose 30 to 40 pounds or more on fad diets will gain it all back (often with interest) within 1 year. And 99 percent will have gained back all the lost weight within 3 years.

The Trouble with Diets

There are many reasons why most fad diets don't work in the long run:

+ They're generally poorly conceived and based on wishful thinking. They blame "nutrimatic food allergies" or praise "reverse metabolic enhancing foods," neither of which exist.

+ They often single out a few food "heroes" or food "villains." Gorging yourself on one "slimming" food or class of foods is just as useless as blaming a certain food or two for all your weight problems. Developing lifelong good health habits while slimming down requires a well-balanced, well-rounded approach to eating.

✦ They're often crash or semistarvation diets, which can slow your metabolism. When the human body realizes that it's not getting as many calories as before, it wisely downshifts into a lower, slower metabolic gear. The body acts just like a careful accountant who says, "Now that you're earning 25 percent less, you'll have to spend 25 percent less." Once your metabolism has been slowed, it's easier than ever to gain weight again. Crash diets can't work in the long run—but they can certainly harm your health.

✦ They can cause food obsessions by being overly strict. If all of your favorite foods are forbidden, if you always have to count every single calorie, if you must strictly rotate or combine foods, you can become fixated on what you *can't* have. When that happens, it's easy to go off the diet.

✦ They can leave you thinking of yourself as a loser by turning you into a repeat diet customer. So many of my patients have been on more diets than they can count. They continually blame themselves for their failure to lose weight and keep it off. Eventually, their feelings of failure creep into other parts of their lives and they brand themselves losers.

✦ They don't change your habits permanently. They require that you follow a radically different eating plan for a certain amount of time, but make no provision for weight maintenance once you've reached your goal. So you go back to the old eating habits, and the pounds pile right back on.

✦ They may rely on dietary manipulation alone, without incorporating exercise and other helpful habits.

Perhaps worst of all, bad diets can make you sick. In the 1970s, many of the young nurses I knew became ill after going on the liquid protein diets. And I could always count on having one or two patients in the intensive care or the coronary care unit with cardiac arrhythmias due to the use of liquid protein diets and/or diuretics. People also came to the hospital with head injuries sustained when they passed out while on semistarvation diets. It became a routine thing to see patients with heart problems caused by fad diet–induced potassium or magnesium loss, and I saw numerous cases of colitis and diarrhea caused by what we doctors referred to as "fad-dietitis."

At that time, some of my colleagues asked me to examine their secretaries in an effort to discover why they seemed to be constantly fatigued. One surgeon said, "Find out why she keeps walking into doors." The culprit was usually a diet-related metabolic disorder. Some of them were eating nothing but rice or another single food for days and weeks at a time. Now, rice is a perfectly good food, but it does not contain all the nutrients and other substances that we need to thrive. I was actually astonished to see cases of beri-beri, replete with heart failure secondary to nutritional deficits, among the rice-only dieters. (Beri-beri, caused by a lack of vitamin B_1, had been all but eradicated in this country. It took fad diets to bring it back.) Another secretary told me that her new wonder diet consisted of nothing but carrots and enemas! It's no wonder these women became ill.

To Make Matters Worse

There are other reasons why many of us have difficulty losing weight. To begin with, we're bombarded with enticements to eat. Billboards, television commercials, and magazine advertisements constantly encourage us to pig out with their mouthwatering images of delicious-looking, high-fat foods.

To make matters worse, we're eating larger portions than ever before. For example, yesterday's regular order of french fries at McDonald's is today's small. The large fries introduced in 1970 are now called regular. And big has become really *big,* as in the popular "Big Gulp" size soft drinks, which can be as large as half a gallon! Incredibly, many of us seem to have no problem gulping down all that food, because we are lucky enough not to suffer from bad teeth, incurable stomach ulcers, various gastrointestinal infections, or other ailments that might keep us from eating our fill.

Perhaps worst of all, evolution works against us. We were genetically programmed to want to eat more than we needed when food was abundant. This way, we could build up reserves for times when food was scarce. That's why we have a tendency to store up excess fat and hang on to it tenaciously. In fact, our bodies are willing to part with those fat reserves only if we are close to starvation. The "saddle bags" on the upper thighs and/ or the fatty bulges on the underside of the buttocks are especially difficult to reduce.

Why Do I Love Food?

There are many theories to explain how the brain regulates food intake. One argues that there are two separate entities located in the hypothalamus (a small part of the brain). One is the feeding center and the other the satiety center. The feeding center sends out a signal to eat when your body requires nourishment, and the satiety center shuts down the appetite when you've had enough. Studies have shown that if you stimulate a laboratory animal's feeding center, it will eat. On the other hand, if the animal's feeding center is damaged or destroyed, it loses its appetite.

Another theory proposes that certain hormones are responsible for telling the brain when you've had enough to eat. The interaction of food and the stomach prompts the release of a hormone or group of hormones that travel to the brain and turn off the appetite. A gastrointestinal hormone called CCK (cholecystokinin) may be one of these "I'm full" hormones. Indeed, animals injected with CCK stop eating.

Is There an Answer?

If we cannot manage to eat less in the long run, and we are lucky enough never to have to face starvation, how can we avoid gaining weight?

One answer lies in products like Olestra. This is a "fat" that cooks and tastes like any other fat but the body cannot assimilate because its molecules are too large to be absorbed into the bloodstream through the walls of the stomach and intestines. Instead, it passes right through the gastrointestinal tract. For example, if we consume potato chips made with Olestra, they taste generally the same as the regular chips and the potato portion is absorbed by the body in the regular way. However, the Olestra passes through our bodies without adding to our fat buildup.

But, of course, we cannot make every fatty product with Olestra. Meat contains its own fat. So do nuts, olives, avocados, and a thousand other foods. When we eat them, we are forced to eat fat. Moreover, if we eat out, we are fed huge quantities of fat of which we may not even be aware. Many salad dressings contain as much fat in a single serving as we need all day. Dishes such as scrambled eggs get as much as half their calories from fat. Chocolate is mostly fat. A Quarter Pounder with cheese contains about 28 grams of fat. And remember, a gram of fat has more than twice the calories of carbohydrates.

Another solution is to take one of the several popular new prescription drugs that inhibit appetite. The two most popular are Redux and its predecessor, Phen-Fen (named for the combination of the drugs phentermine and fenfluramine). Both Redux and Phen-Fen work by speeding up the mechanisms by which our brains normally tell us we are full and should stop eating. Specifically, they signal the neurons in the brain. The "Phen" part increases norepinephrine and dopamine, and the "Fen" increases serotonin in extra large quantities. The serotonin works on the receptors of adjacent neurons to inform the brain that our stomach is full before it really is. In this way, the feeling of hunger and the desire for food is cut off and people quit eating much sooner than they would naturally.

In principle, there is nothing wrong with this approach. In practice, however, there seem to be rather large risks attached. For example, an article in the September 1996 issue of *The New England Journal of Medicine* suggests that the likelihood of primary pulmonary hypertension, a dangerous disease of the blood vessels in the lungs and heart, rises from 2 to 46 cases per million after 3 months of Phen-Fen usage. While this is still a minor risk, it is illustrative of the potency of these drugs, and certainly suggests that they are not harmless. Even Redux, which seems to be milder than Phen-Fen, is known to cause fatigue, diarrhea, unpleasant dreams, and daytime mood swings.

In net, while these drugs are probably better than morbid obesity, they are not the ideal solution for those of us who are 10 to 50 pounds overweight. We would certainly feel and look better, have more energy, live longer and healthier, and enjoy our lives more if we lost those unneeded pounds. But it's hardly worth risking brain damage, unlikely though it may be. And it's even doubtful whether we are prepared to put up with headaches, diarrhea and permanently dry mouths (all occasional side effects of Redux) for the sake of a few lost pounds.

We Can Block Fat—Forever

Americans spend more than *$30 billion* every year on weight-loss foods, clinics, books, pills, surgeries, exercise plans, diet sodas, and gimmicks, but we're still an obese nation. What we've been doing is clearly not working. The statistics show—as most of us have observed for ourselves—that weight gain over time is almost inevitable. Fad diets don't work, medicines and other gimmicks don't help us.

Diets don't work; we're genetically programmed to eat more than we need. We're just stuck with the problem, right?

Wrong!

For years I've had a great deal of success helping patients lose weight with my 8-Point Fat Blocker Program. It's not a faddish diet and it's not a gimmick; it really works. The program helped many of my patients control their weight and, equally important, reduce their fat intake. This, in turn, helps to control their cholesterol and blood fats, reduce their risk of heart disease and cancer, and otherwise brighten their health outlook.

The Fat Blocker Program, combining healthful eating with exercise and positive thinking, is based on the safe and sane principles that have won praise from medical experts all across the country. It also has something extra, a little lift to help get people started and keep them going through difficult periods. That something is Chitosan. For each gram (1,000 mg) of Chitosan that you take before a fatty meal, three to six grams of fat will pass through your body undigested. That fat won't contribute calories, and it won't increase your cholesterol or blood fat levels. It's as if it were never there.

The Fat Blocker Program does not make outrageous claims. You will *not* lose 30 pounds in two weeks while gorging on cake and ice cream. Instead, you will improve your health as you safely, steadily drop down to your ideal weight and stay there. I've seen it happen—many times.

I was horrified when Jan, a 45-year-old math teacher in Los Angeles, told me about the diet she was following. "I'm 5' 3", 198 pounds and still gaining. Right now I'm eating nothing but pineapple, rice, and carrots," she admitted sheepishly. "I've been on every diet, but not for long. I just can't stick with it. But I have to try or soon I'm going to be wider than I am tall. Look at this picture of me drawn by one of my fourth graders." She showed me a crayon drawing of a bowling ball with a little head, arms and legs. It was labeled "Mrs. Bowling Ball."

"Why do you think you can't stick with a diet?" I asked.

"I love chocolate too much," she replied. "And I love the taste of ice cream, cake, pie."

Jan's problem was common. How do you stick to a sensible but strict diet? It has to be sensible, otherwise you'll jeopardize your health. But if it's too strict, there's too much temptation to break the rules. That's where Chitosan comes in handy. It allows you the occasional splurge that helps you stay on the Fat Blocker Program, but minimizes the consequences by preventing your body from absorbing much of the excess fat. The psychological desire for a treat is reconciled with the physiologic need to keep your fat intake low. You can't quite have your cake and eat it too, but you *can* quench the desire for "forbidden foods" that pushes so many of us off our diets and undoes all of our hard work.

I told Jan about the Fat Blocker Program. When she tried it, she began losing weight almost immediately and for the first time ever she was able to stick with a diet. "My successes were like a snowball rolling down a hill, getting bigger and bigger. Only I was getting smaller, not bigger. Each month I lost more than the month before. And I could stick to the diet because once a week I could have something like a hot fudge sundae. The Chitosan made it possible for me to eat the foods I love without ballooning up again. Since I wasn't breaking my diet, I didn't feel guilty and I didn't start stuffing myself like I used to. It's been great."

Then she showed me another picture that she had confiscated from the "artist" in her fourth grade class. "This time he drew me as a bowling pin, not a bowling ball. That's a lot better." She laughed. "When I lose 30 more pounds, he probably won't want to draw any more pictures of me. I'll be too normal-looking."

One of the earliest Fat Blocker success stories was Bob, a 45-year-old, 320-pound computer programmer who had been grossly obese for many years. "I had a little belly when I left college," Bob explained, "then love handles, then what I call my belly bib. I call it that because the fat hanging from my belly completely covers my belt and protects it from, well, the elements, I guess."

As Bob's belly expanded, his life contracted. By his early thirties he was spending most of his time either working, playing with his computer, or lying on the couch watching television. "I really don't mind being fat, Dr. Fox," he explained when he first came to my office. "That's just me. But when these chest pains started, I knew I had to do something. I'm really afraid I'm going to have a heart attack and die, because that's what happened to both my father and grandfather. They got fat and died of heart attacks before they were 50."

Bob made the rounds of doctors' offices, trying one medicine after another for his chest pains and elevated blood pressure. Both of these conditions were caused by his high-fat, high-cholesterol diet, his completely sedentary lifestyle, and the 150 extra pounds he carried in his "belly bib," chest, and rear end. Meanwhile, he continued gaining weight. "The medicines aren't doing it for me, Doctor. I don't want to die, so I've got to lose weight."

I put him on the Fat Blocker Program, not sure if it would really work for someone that morbidly obese. To be on the safe side I also had him continue with the medicines for his heart and blood pressure. But as the weeks passed and Bob steadily lost weight, I began to relax. The pounds seemed to melt away, his chest pains disappeared, and both his cholesterol and blood pressure dropped back down toward safe levels. As his health improved, I gradually began phasing out his medicines. Finally, even his belly bib disappeared and we could actually see his belt again! He had lost 130 of that excess 150 pounds, bringing his weight down to a relatively safe (if slightly pudgy) 190.

Two years later, Bob was still at a normal weight and still healthy. "I think I ate because I was scared of dying, like my father and grandfather," he told me. "Now that I'm at a normal weight, I'm not afraid of dying anymore so I'm not scarfing everything in sight. And I feel like grabbing a candy bar occasionally, but well, the Chitosan helps take care of that."

Remember Claire, the computer-savvy nurse who used her diet database to track her failure on numerous diets? She showed me her revised diet graph not too long ago. "These lines track my progress on the diets," she explained, pointing to the various colored, solid, dashed, and dotted lines on the screen. "This one is Atkins, this one is the Scarsdale, this one is the liquid protein, and so on. Now this one," she continued, pointing to a bright red line, "is your Fat Blocker Program. See how my weight moves down, and then stays down all the way across the screen? Each of these marks is one month and the red line stays down for 30 of them, so it's been 2$^1/_2$ years that I've kept the weight off!"

Jan, Bob, and Claire are just three of the many people who have successfully blocked their fat. You can do it, too, by following the simple eating and exercise plans that I'll describe in coming chapters, and maintaining a positive attitude toward your weight, your health, and life in general. You'll learn how to safely use Chitosan to help you get started, stick with the program and get through any rough periods. But before delving into the specifics of Chitosan and the Fat Blocker Program, let's take a look at the dangers of excess fat.

2

What's Wrong with Excess Weight?

"So I'm fat, big deal," the 32-year-old disc jockey for a local radio station exclaimed when I told him that he was obese. "I never go to the beach so I don't care if I've got a fat stomach. Hey, I work in radio, no one ever sees me. So what's the big deal?"

If aesthetics or the inability to fit into a seat at the movie theater were the only problems associated with obesity, being overweight wouldn't be much more than a cosmetic problem or an occasional inconvenience. But excess body fat and blood fats are more damaging than that—much more. They can cause or increase the risk of heart disease, stroke, cancer, hypertension, immune system weakness, osteoarthritis, diabetes, gallstones, and other problems.

When I was growing up during the Great Depression, we admired voluptuous, Rubenesque women and men with prominent, protruding abdomens. Their weight was a sign of prosperity and seemed to suggest good health to us. (We called a pot belly an alderman's belly because these officials always seemed to be portly and always seemed to have money. Theirs were socially approved bodies.) But since that time we've learned a lot about the effects of fat on health. We now know that being obese, or simply overweight, raises the odds of contracting various diseases. For example, a study of 115,000 American women, ages 35–55, showed that being 5 percent or so above ideal body weight made one 30 percent more likely to develop coronary artery disease, while being 30 percent over ideal body weight led to a whopping 300 percent in the risk of this disease. I've observed this same correlation in thousands of patients. Losing weight and losing fat has almost always helped my heart patients.

High blood pressure (hypertension) is also related to excess fat. A major cause of stroke and heart failure, high blood pressure is endemic here in the United States. We doctors pass out pill after pill in an apparently futile attempt to control blood pressure, which often goes unnoticed because it may produce no symptoms—until that first stroke, heart attack, or bout of heart failure. I remember well a 67-year-old man named Sam who came to see me after having been to several other physicians. Before this former marine colonel even sat down in my office, he began telling me of his ills: "I have high blood pressure and congestive heart failure. My legs are swollen. I get dizzy spells and feel tired all the time. The pills the doctors gave me, all six of them, are ruining what little life I have left in me. Can you help?"

At 210 pounds, Sam was carrying about 50 pounds of extra weight. I told him that if he followed the Fat Blocker Program he would feel better, get healthier, be able to get rid of most or all of his medicines, and lose about 50 pounds. "But it's up to you," I told the ex-soldier, looking him straight in the eye. "I'm giving you responsibility for your health. I'm giving you the power to cure yourself. Are you up to it?" (I especially enjoyed challenging this colonel, for I had only been a lowly buck private when I was in the army!)

"Doc, consider it done."

Six months later he had completely changed his diet, lost much of the excess weight, and exercised regularly. He felt a thousand percent better and looked great. My examination and the laboratory studies confirmed that he was as healthy as he felt and no longer needed his medicines. There was no magic involved in this case, it was a simple matter of losing excess fat.

It's not just the heart and circulation that suffer from excess fat on the body or in the blood. As any doctor who has treated osteoarthritis can tell you, obesity makes joint pain a good deal worse, especially if the arthritic joint is a weight-bearing one such as the ankle, knee, hip, or spine. One of the quickest and safest ways to markedly improve the pain and disability of osteoarthritis is simply to get the patients to lose weight. For most people, arthritis care begins with weight loss.

I've also noticed that low back pain is especially prevalent in people who have "apple" shapes, with their excess fat stored in and around their belly and abdomen. All that weight in the abdomen causes the center of gravity to change, affecting both the position and posture of their back. This, in turn, can lead to back pain. Many times, I have been able to help patients ease back pain to the point where they could throw away their pain medications just by helping them lose weight. Excess weight in the chest and upper back can also make breathing difficult, which is why so many overweight people are short of breath (dyspnea) after just a little exertion.

Heart disease, hypertension, osteoarthritis, back pain, difficulty breathing, and we've only begun to discuss the ill effects of excess fat. For example, did you know that skin disorders are more common in the obese? One reason is that sweating increases due to the extra insulation that fatty tissue provides. (This sweating can be especially heavy after eating.) Sweat can get trapped in the thick skin folds and become a medium for pathogenic bacteria, leading to skin infections. Skin maceration, pain, and discomfort can also occur as the obese person's arms and legs rub against the flanks and thighs when walking. Swelling of the feet, ankles, and lower legs, which is common in the obese, can lead to the breakdown of skin and further pain.

Obesity is also a major cause of diabetes mellitus Type II, which we used to call adult-onset diabetes. This devastating disease can lead to blindness, strokes, heart attacks, gangrene, kidney failure, and infections. Yet often it can be eliminated simply by losing the extra pounds.

So there is no doubt about it—obesity is a dangerous condition. In fact, it is a risk factor for 4 of the 7 leading causes of death in the United States. But before delving further into the hazards of excess body fat, let's define a few important terms.

Obesity, Overweight, Blood Fats, and Cholesterol

Obesity, simply put, is carrying too much fatty tissue in the body. Too much is defined as 20 percent greater than the ideal weight given in the standard height/weight tables, such as the one below.

Overweight, on the other hand, means weighing more than the number of pounds recommended for your height and body build. Just being overweight doesn't necessarily imply a health risk. What's far more important is whether or not you're overfat, and you can't determine that simply by stepping on the scale. The most accurate way to determine whether you are overweight or obese (or neither of these) is to have your body fat measured. (Of course there are some pretty obvious indications of overweight and obesity—a prominent belly, excessively large, squishy-looking thighs, double chins, etc.)

The fat in our blood is different from the fat stored in our bellies, thighs, or extra chins. Stored fat represents extra calories, which we might have consumed as fat, protein, or carbohydrates. Blood fats, on the other hand, are active fats that are being transported throughout the body to perform specific duties. And in order to get to where they're going, triglycerides and cholesterol, the two major kinds of blood fats, have to hitch a ride on proteins. These fat-protein combinations are called *lipoproteins* and there are several different kinds. The high-density lipoproteins (HDL) bind up cholesterol and carry it to the liver where it is disposed of. The higher the HDL level, the better for

SUGGESTED WEIGHTS
(without shoes or clothing)

**The lower numbers in the ranges apply to women,
the higher numbers to men.**

Height	Ages 19–34	Ages 35 and over
5'0"	97–128	108–138
5'1"	101–132	111–143
5'2"	104–137	115–148
5'3"	107–141	119–152
5'4"	111–146	122–157
5'5"	114–150	126–162
5'6"	118–155	130–167
5'7"	121–160	134–172
5'8"	125–164	138–178
5'9"	129–169	142–183
5'10"	132–174	146–188
5'11"	136–179	151–194
6'0"	140–184	155–199
6'1"	144–189	159–205
6'2"	148–195	164–210
6'3"	152–200	166–216
6'4"	156–205	173–222

Taken from "Suggested Weights For Adults," Dietary Guidelines for Americans, U.S. Dept. of Agriculture and Health and Human Services, 1990.

your health because it helps to keep the arteries clean. The low-density lipoproteins (LDL) carry cholesterol to the walls of the arteries and deposit it there, therefore the lower your LDL levels the better. The very low density lipoproteins (VLDL) and the chylomicrons carry the triglycerides from the intestine into the blood system. Once in the tiny blood vessels of the muscle and fatty tissue, 90 percent of the chylomicron triglycerides are taken out of the circulation by enzymes called lipases. Thanks to the lipases, some of the fat we eat is used for energy, while the rest is stored in fat cells.

Although they are not the same thing, cholesterol is linked to fat. Technically speaking, cholesterol is a fat-soluble steroid alcohol made by the body and used to make cell membranes, sex hormones, and cortisone, among other things. Our bodies make some 500–1,000 milligrams of this substance daily, which is all the cholesterol we need. We really don't need to get any cholesterol in our diets, but of course we do. We take in cholesterol whenever we eat meat, fish, chicken, eggs, milk, or other foods that come from animals. And many of these foods are also high in fat. Foods that come from plants, however, such as fruits, vegetables, grains, peas, beans, and lentils, do not contain cholesterol and, with a few exceptions, are also low on fat.

Most of us take in 400–500 milligrams of cholesterol every day in the food that we eat. The body may attempt to compensate for this additional load by cutting back on its own cholesterol production. When, as often happens, the body cannot cut back far enough, the blood cholesterol level rises. Eating saturated fats also causes the body to manufacture cholesterol. In fact, you could eat no animal foods at all but still cause your blood cholesterol to rise by eating foods made with palm and/or coconut oil, both of which are high in saturated fat.

As a rule of thumb, you can simultaneously lower your fat intake and cholesterol level by eating more vegetables, fruits, and whole grains. On the other hand, consuming more meat and high-fat dairy products will cause both of these levels to rise.

Now that we know what obesity, overweight, cholesterol,

and blood fats are, let's see how an excess of any or all of these can be harmful to your health.

Fat, Cholesterol, and Heart Disease

The heart, a simple mechanical wonder, beats some 100,000 times per day, perhaps 3 billion times over a lifetime. Every 60 seconds, the heart pumps out between 5 and 6 quarts of blood. In order to continue beating, the heart muscle needs a continuous supply of energy, which it gets from oxygen in the blood. The heart muscle is fed by an uninterrupted supply of fresh blood flowing through its own tiny arteries (called the coronary arteries because they seem to sit, like a crown, atop the heart muscle). But if that flow of oxygenated blood is cut off, the results can be disastrous.

What Should the Numbers Be?

There is no doubt that the risk of coronary heart disease rises as the cholesterol increases. Conversely, the risk drops as cholesterol falls. Although the American Heart Association recommends that the total cholesterol be 200 or less, I feel that this is too high. It may be average, but being average in this country is a risky proposition. After all, the average person with the average cholesterol gets the average heart attack or stroke. Being average isn't healthy. We want to be better than average—much better.

I tell my patients that we should aim for ideal cholesterol and fat numbers, not average. It may not be possible for all of us to have ideal numbers, but we should know what we're striving for. Here are the ideals:

+ Total cholesterol—150, or no more than 100 plus your age
+ LDL "bad" cholesterol''—100 or less
+ HDL "good" cholesterol—55 plus
+ VLDL cholesterol—20 or less
+ Triglycerides—less than 100

Most of what we call heart disease is really coronary heart disease, or problems with the coronary arteries that tunnel through the heart muscle to deliver fresh blood. Imagine throwing a little rubber ball into the plumbing system in your house. Sooner or later the ball will lodge in a small pipe, stopping the flow of water. Any fixture downstream of the ball will dry up from lack of water. Now imagine a tiny ball (a blood clot or a piece of plaque) in your arteries, drifting through the larger arteries with no problem. The coronary arteries bringing blood to the heart muscle are very small. If the ball tries to drift through these arteries it may get stuck, blocking the flow of blood and killing all portions of the heart muscle that are downstream of the blockage. This is commonly known as a heart attack.

Blockages in the coronary arteries, which are quite common, are caused by many factors, including high blood pressure, high blood fats, stressful living, obesity, lack of exercise, cigarette smoking, and diabetes mellitus. Excess cholesterol, elevated blood fat, and obesity are among the most dangerous of the risk factors.

As excess cholesterol in the bloodstream flows through the body's arteries, some of it binds permanently to the walls of the coronary and other arteries. More bits of cholesterol, plus fat and debris from the bloodstream, may join the buildup on the wall, eventually creating a lump inside the artery. This cholesterol/fat lump may continue to grow until the artery is completely blocked, triggering a heart attack. (Imagine a small car stuck on the side of the freeway. Traffic flows smoothly until another car smacks into the first, then another and another, creating a pileup. Now traffic is slow, but cars are still able to get through. Unfortunately, more and more cars join the pileup until the freeway is completely blocked and no cars can get through. Something similar can happen in the arteries, with cholesterol, fat, and debris taking the place of the cars.)

In other cases, a small blood clot which has formed in another part of the body may drift into the partially blocked artery and get stuck at the lump, blocking the blood flow. This occurs more often in the brain than the heart. (That would be like a large truck getting stuck in a small tunnel, preventing any other cars from getting through.) Heart attacks can also be caused by stress-related arterial spasms. Muscles surrounding the coronary arteries may suddenly go into spasm and clamp down, stopping the blood flow. If an artery has already been narrowed by cho-lesterol/fat plugs, a minor spasm can be a major disaster.

Like cholesterol, fat participates in the making of the lumps that can clog arteries and block the flow of blood. And it has another way of causing trouble for the heart. If you have some-one eat a very high-fat meal, draw a sample of their blood, set the blood in a test tube, and sit down to watch, you'll eventually see the fat from the blood rise to the top of the tube, as the fat did in milk bottles in the days before milk was homogenized. It will be obvious; it's the sludgy stuff. That same sludge clogs up your bloodstream, turning fluid that flows easily through the pipes, and some of the things in that fluid, into, well, sludge. For example, the red blood cells that carry oxygen are normally able to move easily through these blood vessels. But as the fat from the food gets into the bloodstream, the blood cells slush to-gether, looking like a stack of coins. This is called the *rouleau* effect. Up to nine hours later, the blood cells may still be stuck together in misshapen clumps in the tiny blood vessels. How well can the red blood cells carry out their jobs when they're bent out of shape and stuck together? Not very well. That's why 4 or 5 hours after a fatty meal, when the blood fat levels have risen quite a bit, certain people have chest pains, abnormal EKGs, and possibly heart attacks. The fat also prevents the re-lease of a substance called nitrous oxide, which relaxes and di-lates the arteries.

I sometimes draw blood from my patients, then show them how milky and sludgy their blood looks (instead of fluid). I also have them look at a drop of their blood through a special dark-field microscope. They can see how their blood is filled with "snow," which are white patches of fat. Later, after they've adopted a low-fat diet, they can see how clear and fluid their blood looks. It's a great motivator.

Fat and Cancer

Back in the early 1980s, the United States government reported that cancer is related to what we do or do not eat. In a 2-year, 1-million-dollar, 445-page study, the National Academy of Sciences validated what many nutritionally minded physicians had been saying for years: There is a definite link between diet and health. In their study, *Diet, Nutrition, and Cancer*, the Academy concluded that eating certain food-stuffs can increase, or decrease, the incidence of cancer.

More than 1,000 Americans die of cancer every day. Simple dietary changes may prevent an estimated 60 percent of those cancer deaths in women, and 40 percent in men. In other words, roughly half of those 1,000-plus deaths each and every day can be prevented by diet.

The exact mechanisms by which diet alters the path of cancer remain shrouded in mystery. But we do know that there are at least two steps involved: initiation and activation.

The nucleus of every cell in your body contains DNA. Short for deoxyribonucleic acid, DNA is a specialized protein that serves as the instruction manual telling each and every cell what to do and how to do it. Your DNA is also your body's "master plan," ensuring that all the cells in your body work in concert to promote health and well-being.

A normal cell is initiated into a cancerous mode when a carcinogen (a cancer-causing agent) alters the cell's DNA. In other words, the carcinogen rewrites the cell's instruction manual. Any number of things can be carcinogens, including fat, certain substances in foods, chemicals, ultraviolet light, and radiation. The newly initiated cell is harmless—at first. It may remain dormant for minutes, days, years, or decades. In fact, it's quite likely that many of your body cells are initiated. But you don't know they're there because they're not bothering you. And they won't bother you unless they're activated, or given the go signal. Activators wake up the sleeping initiated cell, turning it malignant. Activated, malignant cells can multiply without restraint, using the nutrients in your body to grow beyond the bounds of reason, crowding, invading, and strangling parts of your body.

What substances can activate a dormant initiated cell? We have identified many activators, and there are undoubtedly others. One that we all come in contact with is dietary fat. Fat is both an initiator and an activator.

Fat's ability to activate cancer of the colon and rectum was probably first demonstrated in 1967, when a study by Ernst Wynder noted that:

1. The incidence of cancer of the colon and rectum was low in Japan.
2. The traditional Japanese diet is low in fat (only about 10 percent of its calories come from fat).
3. The children of Japanese who immigrated to this country adopted our high-fat American diet.
4. They also suffered from a tremendous increase in the incidence of colon and rectum cancer.

You can see the evolution of disease risk by tracing its rise as people move and change diets. For example, Japanese women living in Japan have one-fifth the incidence of breast cancer that American women do. When Japanese women move to the United States their incidence of breast cancer remains low. But it begins to rise for their daughters, who often adopt a mixed traditional Japanese–modern American diet. The incidence of the disease rises even more for their granddaughters, who are often completely Americanized and eating our unhealthful fare with gusto.

Similar studies have been performed on other populations. The results are the same: When you move to this country and adopt our high-fat diet, you also tend to adopt our diseases. As an internist and cardiologist with over 40 years of experience, I have had the opportunity to treat a great number of immigrant families from Japan, China, Mexico, and other countries. I noticed that the elderly immigrants who continued to eat their traditional, low-fat diet were often much healthier than their native-born children and grandchildren, who relished the standard high-fat diet we eat in this country.

I remember one patient, a pleasant Japanese-American man. By age 48 he had had three heart attacks and was unable to work. His brother had died of a heart attack at age 45, and a sister had had a serious heart attack when she was 50. But the problem was not genetic. There was no history of heart disease in their family and their parents, both in their late 70s, were in excellent health. The difference between the parents and their children and grandchildren was mostly in their respective diets. The elderly parents continued to eat the traditional low-fat, high–complex carbohydrate Japanese diet. The children and grandchildren were living off—and dying from—the fat of the land.

The damage done by the standard fat-laden American diet can be horrifying. Forty to 50 percent of its calories come from fats. When you consume that much fat, large amounts of bile acids are secreted into your intestines to help emulsify, or break down, the fat particles. These bile acids and their breakdown products are excellent activators. The more fat you eat, the more activators you release into your system.

As both a cancer initiator and activator, fat is one of the reasons why we who live in the United States and other affluent nations suffer from the cancers of affluence. These are cancer of the breast, ovaries, and uterus in women; cancer of the pancreas and prostate in men; and cancer of the colon and rectum in both sexes. The National Cancer Institute believes that approximately 60 percent of cancer deaths in women and some 40 percent of cancer deaths in men can be attributed directly or indirectly to the standard, high-fat American diet.

Scientific Proof for the Cancer-Fat Link

The scientific literature is filled with studies confirming the relationship between fat and cancer. For example:

+ **Breast cancer**—From the *Journal of the American Medical Association* comes a report[1] pointing out that information from animal experiments and human correlation studies strongly supports the hypothesis that dietary fat causes breast cancer.

+ **Breast cancer**—From the *Journal of the National Cancer Institute* comes a review[2] of information taken from 12 case-controlled studies. The authors of the review conclude that the rate of postmenopausal breast cancer could be cut some 25 percent if fat intake was reduced.

+ **Breast and colon cancer**—A 1991 study[3] reported in the *American Journal of Clinical Nutrition* reported that "Evidence relating dietary fat to cancer at sites such as the breast and colon is provided by experiments showing that animals fed high-fat diets develop cancer at these sites more readily than do animals fed low-fat diets, and by epidemiological data from different countries showing strong positive correlations between cancer incidence and mortality, and level of dietary fat. . . . The weight of evidence continues to indicate that long-term adherence to a low-fat diet can reduce the risk of some common types of cancer."

+ **Colon cancer**—A prospective study involving 88,751 women ranging in age from 34–59, found a positive association between dietary fat and the risk of colon cancer.[4]

+ **Colon cancer**—When the past lifestyles of 906 Chinese patients with colorectal cancer were compared to those of 2,000 controls, researchers found a strong link between intake of saturated fat and the cancer. Those who ate the most saturated fat were 4 times as likely to be stricken as those who ate the least.[5]

+ **Ovarian cancer**—For this study,[6] the dietary histories of 455 Italian women suffering from ovarian cancer were compared to those of 1,385 controls. A high-fat diet was found to be the riskiest, while one filled with green vegetables, whole grains, fish, and carrots offered the most protection.

This evidence associating excessive fat intake to various forms of cancer is overwhelming. On the one hand, that's bad news. But on the other hand it's good news, for it points us toward an easy solution. We have the wonderful opportunity to help reduce the incidence of cancer for ourselves, our loved ones, and all of society simply by reducing the amount of fat we take, and keep, in our bodies.

Fat and Hypertension

We get fat in our diet from four sources:

+ Saturated fat from beef, pork, lamb, veal, butter, milk, cheese, eggs, and other foods that come from animals. Coconut and chocolate are also high in saturated fat, as are margarine, cocoa butter, and palm oil.

+ Polyunsaturated fats, which come from fish, poultry, vegetables, and vegetable oils (such as corn oil). Polyunsaturated fats are more fluid at room temperatures.

+ Monounsaturated fats, found in olives and olive oil.

+ Hydrogenated fats. These are fats or oils taken from vegetables and then artificially converted into solid shortening or margarine by adding hydrogen to them. In this process polyunsaturated fats are converted to saturated fats.

The fats from our foods get into our bloodstream, where they can cause the red blood cells to clump together. This can severely reduce the blood flow and oxygen exchange in certain parts of the body, leading to angina (chest pain) or a heart attack if the oxygen exchange is totally cut off. And if the arteries are not already clogged, they can become so as the fat we eat is deposited onto the artery walls. The accumulation of plaque in the artery walls makes these pipes narrower and more rigid. It's harder for the heart to pump blood through these narrowed, rigid pipes. It takes more pressure to keep the blood moving, and so the heart has to work harder.

In medical school we learned a simple formula: Blood Pressure = Cardiac Output × Peripheral Resistance. This means that blood pressure will increase if the heart works harder to keep the blood flowing through the body, or if the blood vessels put up more resistance to the flow of blood by becoming, for example, more narrow. With the heart pumping harder to push blood through narrowed arteries, with both the cardiac output and the peripheral pressure up, the blood pressure rises. It's simple mathematics.

Consuming a high-fat diet that "thickens" the blood and clogs the arteries pushes the blood pressure up, often to dangerously high levels. There are medicines to handle the situation, but they sometimes have serious side effects. The best, safest, natural, and most permanent solution is to clean out your arteries and thin your blood by adopting my Fat Blocker Program. You can also often reduce the risk of elevated arterial pressure by losing weight. This is another way of lowering the risk of suffering or dying from cardiovascular disease.[7]

I've seen the beneficial effects of the Fat Blocker Program on elevated blood pressure many times. In fact, one of my early successes was with my longtime friend Dick, who one day discovered that his blood pressure had shot up to 195/115 as his waistline ballooned to 42. His personal physician put him on beta-blockers and calcium channel blockers, two very powerful medicines. The drugs pushed his pressure down to 130/85, but they also gave him depression, fatigue, vertigo, and impotence. He was given other drugs to deal with those problems, but the second round of medications left the poor 42-year-old feeling weak and more tired than ever. By the time I saw him he said was ready to "drop the damn drugs altogether and take my chances with the high blood pressure."

I convinced Dick to stay with the drugs for just a little while longer, until they could safely be reduced, then eliminated. After 4 months of the Fat Blocker Program, he had lost 40 pounds and was consuming or absorbing significantly less fat than before. His blood pressure dropped down to 120/80, which is normal and healthy. He was able to discard all his medicines, and the unpleasant side effects were soon nothing more than an unhappy, distant memory.

Excess Fat Weakens the Immune System

We're assaulted by viruses, bacteria, and fungi every day; cancer cells arise within our bodies; and other dangers loom. Yet, for the most part, we remain fairly healthy, turning aside most potential illnesses, or weathering the storms when they arise. Our hardiness is due to the tremendous department of defense we all have within our bodies: our immune systems.

T-cells that grapple with invaders in fatal one-on-one combat, giant macrophages that engulf and destroy disease-causing entities, neutrophils that rush lightly armed into battle, B-cells that manufacture antibodies designed to search and destroy specific targets—these are just some of the parts of the mighty immune system.

Like all armies, our immune systems are prepared to operate in many different kinds of terrain. But when the body and blood are filled with fat, the immune system is hampered. Imagine that you're a foot soldier or tank driver having to slog through sticky, knee-deep mud, or the captain of a boat crashing its way through an ice field. That's something like the difficulties our immune system soldiers face when our bodies are filled with fat. Excessive amounts of fats, especially polyunsaturated fatty acids and cholesterol, have been linked to a weakening of the immune system.[8] Excess blood fats directly interfere with immune system cells,[9] the lymphocytes, T4 and T8 cells, B-cells, natural killer cells, monocytes, and giant macrophages. Fat also impairs the ability of the red blood cells to deliver oxygen to immune system tissues that depend on a good supply of oxygen and nutrients in order to keep us healthy. Meanwhile, studies have shown that cutting your fat intake to lower levels may make your natural killer cells more effective,[10] all the more reason to keep our fat intake low.

Excess fat may be more dangerous to us than many of the viruses and bacteria that we come in contact with. In over 40 years of treating patients, I have observed that people eating very high fat diets tend to get more infections, and have a more difficult time healing, than those who do not. That's why I say that cutting our fat intakes down to safe levels can be powerful medicine.

Fat and Arthritis

Arthritis is a very common ailment, afflicting tens of millions of Americans. There are many types of arthritis, including rheumatoid arthritis, gouty arthritis, bursitis, systemic infections arthritis, and osteoarthritis. The most common form of the disease, osteoarthritis results from a breakdown of the cartilage that normally cushions the ends of the bones and prevents them from rubbing against each other and wearing away. If the cartilage does wear away, the result can be stiffness, pain, loss of joint mobility, and deformation of the joint.

There are many painkillers used to treat arthritis, though none are completely effective. These medicines can help with pain and inflammation, but many of them have side effects. A much simpler approach that I've prescribed with a great deal of success is to slim down. Although obesity does not necessarily cause osteoarthritis, the two often go hand in hand. There is a definite link between gaining weight and developing osteoarthritis, especially in the knees and ankles, which bear the brunt of the extra weight with each step. A large percentage of patients had gained weight shortly before the osteoarthritis began, and some 50 percent of those with the disease had been overweight for 3–10 years before the disease struck.[11]

The Fat Blocker Program has helped many of my arthritis patients get off their medicines while relieving pain and stiffness in their knee, hip, and ankle joints (as have the new developments in arthritis treatment as described in *The Arthritis Cure*, cowritten by Brenda Adderly).

Fat and Diabetes

Instead of saying, "I've got diabetes," some of my patients say, "I've got the sugar." Diabetes in children is caused by the failure of the pancreas to produce sufficient insulin, while adult-onset diabetes is associated with overweight or obesity.

Normally, the carbohydrates we take in from our food are corralled, controlled, and stored by the insulin produced in the pancreas. But sometimes the pancreas is simply unable to produce enough insulin, and the blood sugar runs wild. This condition is known as Type I or insulin-dependent diabetes mellitus. (It used to be called juvenile diabetes.) In other cases, the body produces but has become resistant to its insulin, usually due to obesity, pregnancy, certain drugs, or age. This is known as Type II or noninsulin-dependent diabetes mellitus. (It used to be called adult-onset diabetes.) Diabetes can be a mild annoyance or a major problem. Symptoms include extreme thirst and urination, weight loss despite eating a lot, ulcers, gangrene, and an increased risk of infections, heart disease, kidney failure, stroke, and blindness.

A high-fat diet is one of the most common contributing factors to the development of Type II diabetes. The National Institutes of Health Consensus Development Conference[12] reported that the risk of Type II diabetes rises as body weight increases—and the longer one is obese, the greater the risk. Nearly 80 percent of all those who develop this disease were obese when it struck.

I've been using a low-fat, high–complex carbohydrate, Fat Blocker type of diet for my Type II diabetic patients for well over 20 years, with great success. My clinical experience has been backed up by studies conducted at the University of Kentucky Medical School. There, Dr. James Anderson showed that a tremendous number of diabetics could be helped by switching to the type of diet in my Fat Blocker Program.[13] Not only does my program help those who already have diabetes, it's an excellent preventive measure, as well.

Fat and Gallstones

Many years ago, a group of young medical students, including me, stood by a patient's bed. We listened in awe as the very old doctor/professor, who was probably all of 40 years old, discussed the patient's condition. "Mr. Rapp is a 50-year-old obese man presenting with upper abdominal pain, nausea, vomiting, and bloating, especially after eating fatty foods. We'll conduct an examination and run tests to be sure, but this is the general rule: If an overweight patient has pain in the upper abdomen, think of gallstones."

Gallstones, which we doctors call cholelithiasis, are stones in the gallbladder. Made primarily of cholesterol and bile pigment, they're not cancerous, but they can cause a great deal of trouble. Several things can prompt gallstones, including drinking excessive amounts of alcohol, smoking, and rapid weight loss. The major risk factor is too much fat, whether in the form of too much fat stored in the body or a high-fat, low-fiber diet.

A high-fat, high-cholesterol, low-fiber diet is responsible for about 90 percent of all gallstones. If not treated in time, the stones can lead to infections and rupture the gallbladder. Instead of waiting until after the stones have formed, then submitting to dangerous surgery, medicine, or shock wave therapy (lithotripsy) to break up the stones, it's best to avoid the problem in the first place by staying slim and eating a low-fat diet. Through the years, I have treated many gallstone patients with the low-fat diet, thus avoiding the need for surgery. (I do everything possible to avoid surgery, for every surgery, no matter how "small" or "safe," has complications—including death.)

Excess Fat Is Harmful to Your Health

What's the big deal about being fat? Forget the aesthetics of obesity, it's the health issues that matter. Excess fat, whether stored in the body or floating through the blood system, can lead to heart disease, stroke, diabetes, osteoarthritis, gallstones, difficulty breathing, and a host of other problems. The Fat Blocker Program can help you treat or prevent these ailments by reducing the fat you store and take in. Let's begin our exploration of the program by examining Chitosan.

3

---◆---

The Miracle of Chitosan

In my 40-plus years of practicing medicine, I've seen every kind of diet and diet aid you can imagine. The Alcohol Diet was popular for a while, as were the Scarsdale and Cambridge Diets. There are high-protein diets and liquid diets, diets that tell you to eat all you want and others that leave you feeling starved. There are calorie-counting diets and others that have you dividing foods into categories. Some diets proclaim themselves to be revolutionary, while others boast of their sensibility. Diets have been named for celebrities, cities, foods, and famous hospitals. I've even seen the I Love America Diet, the Never Say Diet diet and other regimens based on slogans.

I've seen a lot of weight-loss ideas, plans, and gimmicks. I've also seen thousands of disappointed patients watch with dismay as the pounds that they thought were gone forever returned to their waists, thighs, hips, chins, and upper arms. But I've never seen anything that can produce results like the Fat Blocker Program, which is spearheaded by Chitosan.

Help from the Simple Shellfish

Back in 1811, a French professor named Henri Braconnot discovered that mushrooms contained a substance called chitin. Technically speaking, chitin is made of many molecules of N-acetyl-D-glucosamine hooked together in a long chain, one after another. Chitin is a natural substance, quite similar to the cellulose found in various plants. Besides mushrooms, it's also found in the shells of crabs, shrimp, and other shellfish.

Other scientists, intrigued by chitin, studied and experimented with it. In 1859, Professor Rouget found that when chitin was "cooked" in alkali, it turned into a slightly different substance called Chitosan. Thanks to the "cooking," the Chitosan is deacetylated, which means that the acetyl parts are pulled away from the chitin molecules, leaving primarily the glucosamine units. These glucosamine units, linked together in a long chain, have positive charges. And those positively charged glucosamine molecules, all lined up and linked together, give Chitosan some amazing properties.

Molecules, like magnets, tend to have positive or negative (+ or −) charges. Molecules with opposite charges are attracted to each other, while those with similar charges (positive and positive, or negative and negative) repel each other. These charges help the molecules decide which other molecules they're supposed to interact with and which to avoid.

Technically Speaking . . .

Both chitin and Chitosan are nitrogenous polysaccharides. Chitosan is synthesized by deacetylating ("cooking") the chitin taken from the exoskeletons of shellfish. (Thus, Chitosan is an alkalized form of chitin.) Chitosan links to fat both electrostatically and hydrophobically. Chitosan is both biocompatible, which means that it's safe to use, and biodegradeable.

Chitosan has a positive charge. Both fatty acids (the building blocks of fat) and bile acids (which are used to make cholesterol) have negative charges, which means that they are naturally attracted to Chitosan. When fatty acids or bile acids come near Chitosan, they grab on and hold tight. Now, instead of fatty acids that can be used to build fat tissue, or bile acids that the body might convert to cholesterol, you have a nondigestible blob that passes right through the intestines and out of the body. The results of many studies make it very clear: Chitosan inhibits the digestion of fat.[1]

Researchers realized that Chitosan had a great deal of potential, and in the early 1900s they devoted a fair amount of time and attention to its study. But when synthetic fibers began appearing in the middle part of the century and synthetic medicines began conquering age-old pestilences, Chitosan was set aside and practically forgotten. It wasn't until the 1970s that scientists took another look at this amazing natural fiber and really began to understand what it could do for us.

Thanks to numerous studies, scientists have discovered that Chitosan has many health-boosting properties. This amazing fiber can

- ✦ Absorb and bind up fat, carrying it through the intestinal tract and out of the body.
- ✦ Guard against heart disease and cancer by lowering blood fat.
- ✦ Increase HDL (the "good" cholesterol).
- ✦ Lower the risk of heart disease, stroke, and other serious ailments.

Although preliminary, there are other promising benefits of Chitosan, which may

- ✦ Guard against gout and some kidney stones by helping to regulate uric acid levels.
- ✦ Speed the healing of wounds and broken bones.
- ✦ Serve as an antacid.
- ✦ Slow the formation of the plaque that causes dental cavities.

Perhaps some of these other advantages will prove to be illusory. But for now, we do know that Chitosan attracts fat and saturated fat and carries it out of the body . . . and that's saying a great deal!

How Does Chitosan Block Fat— and How Well?

Chitosan is a fiber, similar in many respects to the cellulose in foods. But the human body cannot digest Chitosan, so it passes harmlessly through the body. Since the Chitosan is not assimilated by the body, it obviously adds *absolutely no calories to the diet.*

In the stomach Chitosan turns into a gelatin-like substance that grabs on and holds tightly to saturated fat. Stuck in this Chitosan gel by the electrostatic "cling" between its positive charge and the fat's negative charge—very much in the way lint sticks to wool—the fat cannot be absorbed. Instead, it is carried through the upper and lower intestines and right out of the body. It is as if, suddenly, the fat became as nondigestible as Olestra (the new nonabsorbable fat, which recently became available for use in some snack foods). Fat attached to Chitosan has as much impact on the body as fat left on the dining room table!

See for Yourself

The positive electrostatic charge of the Chitosan, the negative charge of saturated fats, and the resulting ability of Chitosan to attract and hold the fat can readily be demonstrated in the laboratory. You can also do a quick and easy experiment in your kitchen. Here's how. Place two cups of hot water into a large glass container, filling the container about half full. Add 1/4 tsp. of melted butter or another liquid saturated fat. Sprinkle about 1/4 gram of Chitosan on the surface of the water, then swirl the water around to spread the Chitosan. In just a short time, you'll see the Chitosan absorbing the fat, forming into lumps that leave the water essentially fat free.

Early impressive evidence that this phenomenon really works came from a series of animal experiments. At least 18 such studies have been conducted at research centers in various countries. The first major study[2] was conducted by J. L. Nauss, J. L. Thompson, and J. Nagyvary of Texas A&M University in 1983. In a carefully controlled project, these three scientists proved that for each gram of Chitosan a group of rats ingested, they excreted 4–5 more grams of fat than the control group.

But since other fibers can also pull dietary fat from the body, some researchers wondered if there was really anything special about Chitosan. Four Japanese scientists[3] used laboratory animals to compare the effects of Chitosan to 22 other fibers, including pectin, guar, carrageen, and others that have been used for weight loss. The animals were divided into 23 groups. During the test period, the groups were fed identical diets, except that each received a different fiber. The amount of food they ate was measured daily, and they were weighed every 3 days. Their feces were collected during the last 3 days of the study period for analysis.

In their 1994 paper describing the results of this study, the researchers reported that "Chitosan markedly increased the fecal lipid excretion and reduced the apparent fat digestibility to about half, relative to the control."[4] In other words, the animals that were given Chitosan digested smaller amounts of the fat that they ate (and more fat exited their bodies with their stool).

These facts looked interesting, but left open the theoretical (although unlikely) possibility that the fat accompanying the Chitosan on its journey out of the body was not fat the animals had eaten, but was instead "pulled" from elsewhere in the body. However, when the researchers analyzed the fat, they confirmed that "the fatty acid composition of the fecal lipids closely reflected that of dietary fat." This essentially proved the point: the theory that Chitosan was indeed binding up the fat that had just been eaten before it could be digested and clog up arteries or cause other trouble. Clearly, the scientists pointed out, this study "suggests that Chitosan specifically inhibited the digestion and absorption of dietary fat."

Let's take a look at some of the numbers from this study. When studying the effects of fiber on dietary fat, researchers looked at several measurable items, including the dry weight of the stool, the total lipid (fat) in the stool, and the apparent digestibility of the fat eaten.

+ The dry weight of the stool should increase as more fat is carried out of the body. In other words, the stool should be bulkier and heavier.

+ Not only should the stool be larger, it should contain a greater percentage of fat.

+ Finally, the apparent fat digestibility should drop. In other words, lower amounts of the fat consumed should be digested as more fat simply passes through the body, making the stool heavier and fattier.

The ideal fat magnet, then, would *increase* the dry weight and total fat content of the feces, while *decreasing* the apparent fat digestibility. And that's exactly what Chitosan did. Here are the results for the top 10 of the 23 fibers in the study:[5]

	Stool: Dry Weight (g/3 days)	Stool: Total Lipid (mg/3 days)	Percent Apparent Fat Digestibility
Chitosan	8.95	5,380.0	50.8
Polyglycol Alginate	5.75	1,641.0	83.4
Carrageen	5.07	1,109.0	90.4
Kapok	7.55	924.0	91.7
Sodium alginate	2.14	727.5	91.9
Pectin	1.22	168.0	92.6
Tragacantha	3.02	837.8	92.8
Guar	1.82	556.5	94.0
Konjak-mannan	1.95	537.9	94.8
Cellulose	4.84	578.8	94.9

The above results would, of course, have slight statistical variations. But their story is so clear that there can be no doubt as to the superior performance of Chitosan.

I've underlined Chitosan's results because the numbers are so impressive. Notice that adding Chitosan to the diet resulted in the heaviest stool collected over a 3-day period (8.95 grams) and the most fat in the stool (5,380 milligrams). That was only to be expected since, as you can see, Chitosan cut the apparent fat digestibility way down—to just about half. The next best performer, Polyglycol Alginate, only cut the fat digestibility down to 80 percent, while the others were all above 90 percent. Clearly, Chitosan was by far the strongest fat magnet in this set of tests. To my knowledge, no other substance has ever been found to get even close to its effectiveness.

Less Fat Equals Less Weight

Of course, animals are not human. Therefore, while the animal studies were conclusive, there was the possibility that the findings did not apply to us.

Fortunately, this possibility has now been removed. The idea that Chitosan can help one lose weight by preventing the absorption of calorie-laden fat is no longer just a theory based on animal studies. It is a fact proved in human studies. It really works. Specifically, a randomized, double-blind study[6] conducted in Finland by Professors Lasus and Abelin in 1994 proved that ingesting Chitosan could help one shed pounds. In this study, 30 obese patients were given Chitosan, while a control group with a precisely identical diet was given a placebo. Within a 4-week period, members of the Chitosan group lost an average of 15 pounds apiece, compared to the placebo group (which only lost 5.5 pounds). The Finnish researchers reported that Chitosan "was the best and most hygenic way to take a weight-reducing substance." They pointed out that it was safe, and their results were in line with those of a 1991 Norwegian trial described below. Both studies were conclusive and very impressive. And I suspect that there is even more good news to come from this remarkable product. What we already know certainly whets the appetite for more research on Chitosan to come.

Research studies conducted under ideal conditions are one thing, but I always want to know how well something works in the real world, where conditions are not always perfect. Fortunately, my patients have enjoyed excellent results with this amazing yet simple substance. I've used Chitosan for years. One of my early Chitosan patients was Joan, a 40-year-old attorney from trendy Brentwood, California. Her ideal weight was 125 pounds and she was frustrated, because even though she'd been dieting conscientiously, she seemed to be stuck at 145. When I first saw her in my office she said, "I want to lose weight, but only in a healthy way. No crazy diets for me."

Since she was already following a highly nutritious, medically safe, low-calorie diet, I felt that she just needed an extra push to get her unstuck. I prescribed Chitosan and she began losing half a pound, then 1 pound a week. "The weight just melted off me," she later reported. "It was easy."

I was glad to see Joan's weight drop down to her ideal range. And I was delighted to note that the Chitosan also pushed up her "good" HDL cholesterol while driving the "bad" LDL cholesterol down. She became slimmer and healthier simultaneously.

John, a 36-year-old entertainment personality, was also pleased with Chitosan's fat-blocking prowess. He lived north of Sunset in Beverly Hills, the choice place to reside in the City of the Stars. "My belly's bulging over my pants, Dr. Fox," he said one day as he slapped his paunch. "I've tried following the diet you told me about, but my schedule is crazy and I'm always eating the junk they bring on the set. Can you help me?"

I measured the circumference of John's abdomen. It was greater than the circumference of his hips. That is a shorthand way I often use for estimating that my patients are at increased risk for heart disease. You can check it out for yourself. If the measurement comes in "backwards" (as one of my patients phrased it), with the abdomen measurement greater than the hip measurement, it's high time you did something about it. In John's case, it was not only that his weight was a health problem, in his business it was an image problem, too. I got him started with Chitosan and the Fat Blocker Program, and soon he was losing weight. After a few months on the program his belly was no longer hanging over his pants, and his abdomen-to-hip ratio shrunk to .75. (This means that the circumference of his abdomen was only 75 percent that of his hips, which is a good indication that patients are safe from heart disease.)

"That did the trick," he told me a few months later in my office, proudly showing me his newly slim waistline. "This has given me the confidence to stick to a healthy diet—forever. No more belly over the pants for me."

Less Fat Also Means Less Heart Disease and Cancer

As you already know, fat is intimately linked to both heart disease and cancer. Fat, especially saturated fat, causes an increase in blood cholesterol, which can lead to sticky deposits on artery walls. These deposits can cause blockages that lead to heart attacks and strokes. The sticky buildup (called atherosclerosis) also increases blood pressure, making it more difficult for the heart to pump blood through the blood vessels.

Additionally, dietary fat plays an important role in the development of cancer. You've already learned this by the example of several generations of families moving from one country to another and watching their children develop cancers of affluence. As you learned in Chapter 2, the cancers of affluence—cancers of the prostate and pancreas for men; colon/rectum cancer for men and women; and cancers of the breast, ovaries, and uterus for women—strike with greater fury in wealthier countries. Here in America, we eat a richer and fattier diet than do our counterparts in poorer countries. It's a well-established fact: Cancer and fat are intimately linked. Therefore, anything that can lower the level of fat in our diets can be a lifesaver.

Chitosan can do just that. Simply by pulling dietary fat out of the body and preventing it from being absorbed into the bloodstream and beyond, Chitosan helps to lower the risk of both heart disease and cancer.

At Least Three to One

While animal studies can be interesting, for real people to use Chitosan in their everyday lives we must put this in perspective. Chitosan, in the simplest terms, does the following:

> For each gram of Chitosan you consume half an hour before a meal, *at least* 3 grams of saturated fat—and as many as 6—will pass through your body undigested.

For simplicity's sake, let's assume that 5 grams of saturated fats pass through the body unabsorbed for every 1 gram of Chitosan that you take. Suppose your dinner normally contains 40 grams of saturated fat (a dangerously high amount). If you take 5 grams of Chitosan before that dinner, the Chitosan can pull away 5×5, or 25 grams of that fat, leaving only 15 to be absorbed by your body. The 25 grams of fat that are attached to the Chitosan pass through your body as if you had not consumed them in the first place.

How helpful is *not* digesting 25 grams of fat? Well, 25 grams of fat contain about 225 calories. If you cut your fat intake by 25 grams, and normally consume 2,000 calories per day, you'll be lowering your calorie intake by 11 percent. And if you use Chitosan before two fatty meals a day, blocking the same amount of fat with each meal, the numbers can double—50 fewer grams of fat digested per day. That comes to 450 calories less, or 22 percent of your daily caloric intake. Not only have you reduced your caloric intake, you've also reduced the danger to your health represented by that excess fat.

Let's look at it from another point of view. According to the Third International Health and Nutrition Examination Survey,[7] the average American consumes 83 grams of fat per day. Using the example above, if you prevent 50 of those fat grams from being absorbed into the body, you reduce your daily fat intake by an impressive 60 percent.

Assuming that every gram of Chitosan pulls 5 grams of fat out of your digestive system, here's how many grams of fat—and calories—you'll avoid if you take Chitosan within half an hour of eating these foods:

Food	Grams of Fat in Food	Add Chitosan	Grams of Fat Actually Digested	Grams of Fat Avoided	Calories Avoided
Jack in the Box Jumbo Jack hamburger	25.6	3 grams	10.6	15	135
Jack in the Box cheese nachos	35.1	3 grams	20.1	15	135
KFC Original Recipe chicken thigh	17.5	3 grams	2.5	15	135
McDonald's English muffin with butter	5.3	1 gram	0.3	5	45
McDonald's Quarter Pounder hamburger	23.5	3 grams	8.5	15	135
Wendy's double hamburger	34	3 grams	19.0	15	135
1 oz. domestic cheddar cheese	9.4	1 gram	4.4	5	45
1 oz. part skim mozzarella cheese	4.5	1 gram	0.0	4.5	45
1 slice apple pie (117 grams)	19.3	3 grams	4.3	15	135

1 slice pecan pie (115 grams)	26.3	3 grams	9.3	15	135
1 croissant (56 grams)	10.8	1 gram	5.8	5	45
1 jelly doughnut (65 grams)	14.3	1 gram	9.3	5	135
1 slice carrot cake (111 grams)	28.1	3 grams	13.1	15	135
1 slice chocolate cheesecake (128 grams)	32.2	3 grams	17.2	15	135
1 Milky Way bar	8	1 gram	3.0	5	45
1 Planter's Peanut Bar	5.4	1 gram	0.4	5	45
1 hard boiled egg (50 grams)	5.6	1 gram	0.6	5	45
1 tbsp. French dressing	6.4	1 gram	1.4	5	45
1 tbsp. Russian dressing	7.8	1 gram	2.8	5	45
1 tbsp. salted butter	11	1 gram	6.0	5	135
1 oz. beef salami	5.7	1 gram	0.7	5	45
3 oz. T-bone steak, choice, broiled	20.9	3 grams	5.9	15	135
4 oz. ham, center slice	14.6	3 grams	0.0	14.6	131
1 cup ice cream (approximately 10% fat)	14.3	1 gram	9.3	5	135

Of course, if you use the more optimistic figure of 6 grams of fat pulled out of the body for each gram of Chitosan taken, the amount of fat and calories saved will be even higher.

Obviously, consuming fewer calories and less fat, while still getting all of the calories and nutrients your body needs, are significant steps toward better health. Chitosan can help you achieve these goals. But don't use it as an excuse to eat even more fatty foods. Obviously, if you make Chitosan the excuse to eat more fat, you will neutralize its positive effects. You may even gain weight. There is no point in taking 3 grams of Chitosan (which will absorb about 9 to 18 grams of fat) and then eating a Big Mac with about 45 grams of fat in it! No, even with Chitosan, a diet that is reasonably low in fat remains an important part of building lifelong health.

Chitosan Helps Keep the Arteries Clean

If Chitosan only blocked the absorption of fat and helped us to lose weight, it would be enough. But it does more. This miraculous substance also alters the blood profile.

There are many tests in a standard blood panel, but two of the most important as far as heart health are concerned are the levels of LDL cholesterol and triglycerides, or blood fats. Elevated levels of LDL cholesterol and triglycerides have both been strongly linked to an increased risk of heart disease. Our livers continuously try to eliminate excess LDL from our bodies by dumping it into our intestines. However, often our livers are not fully successful at eliminating LDL. At other times, a portion of the LDL is reabsorbed through our intestines because we have insufficient fiber to carry it away. Thus, excess LDL, and its concomitants, atherosclerosis and heart disease, are problems faced by millions of people as they age.

To combat excess LDL, doctors prescribe cholestyramine, Mevacor, Zocar or various similar medications. These classes of drugs are effective in reducing LDL, but can cause significant damage to the body. People who take these drugs must be carefully monitored by their physicians.

To a large extent, Chitosan solves the problem of excess LDL because it acts in two ways. First, as stated, it bonds with the fat, thus blocking it from even being absorbed by the body before reaching the liver. At the same time, it acts as a regular dietary fiber and helps carry out any fat that was dumped by the liver into the intestines, avoiding reabsorption. Remarkably, researchers have found in studies comparing Chitosan to cholestyramine that Chitosan is as effective in lowering LDL but, of course, has no known side effects.

The net result of all this is that Chitosan can help reduce the risk of heart disease by lowering the bad cholesterol in our bloodstreams. This was evident as early as 1991, when Norwegian researchers noted that taking Chitosan led to a significant reduction in cholesterol and blood fats.[8] The study put Chitosan's cholesterol-lowering prowess to the test in 8 healthy men ranging in age from 20 to 23 who were given

+ Biscuits (without Chitosan) for the first 6 days of the study,

+ 3 grams of Chitosan baked into biscuits, every day for the next 7 days,

+ 6 grams of Chitosan, via similar biscuits, every day for the ensuing 7 days,

+ Biscuits without Chitosan for the last 7 days of the study

The biscuits looked and tasted alike, so the volunteers did not know when they were getting Chitosan and when they were not.

The results of this "Chitosan Biscuits" study were impressive and again, whet the appetite for more studies. The researchers noted that "When 3–6 grams a day of Chitosan were given in the diet to 8 healthy males, total serum cholesterol significantly decreased. . . ." But when the young men stopped eating the Chitosan biscuits, their cholesterol levels quickly jumped back up to where they had been. Not only that, but the amount of bile acids they excreted *increased* when they ate the Chitosan biscuits. This is important, for the body uses bile acids to make cholesterol. When there are fewer bile acids present, the body manufactures less cholesterol, so pushing out excess bile acids is important for good heart health. (The authors of this study theorized that Chitosan combines with the bile acids, preventing the body from reabsorbing them and using them to synthesize cholesterol. By tying up bile acids in the intestines, Chitosan may also help to reduce the risk of cancer of the colon.)

Chitosan's ability to lower cholesterol in humans is supported by animal studies, including a 1989 study published in the *Journal of Nutrition*[9] in which Chitosan was compared to cellulose and guar gum. Of the 3 fibers under examination, Chitosan "most effectively lowered cholesterol absorption."

But in the study with the 8 young men and the biscuits, Chitosan did more than push down the total cholesterol: It also caused the good HDL cholesterol to rise. HDL (high-density lipoprotein) cholesterol is the helpful cholesterol that carries plaque and debris away from the artery walls and to the liver for disposal. While we want our total cholesterol levels to be low, we want our HDL levels to be high. During the course of this study, Chitosan increased the HDL levels from an average of 51 to 56—a 10 percent increase, which is both significant and healthful.

A Simple Way to View Total Cholesterol and HDL

Generally speaking you want your total cholesterol (TC) to be 150 or less—ideally, it should be 100 plus your age. Your HDL should be 50 or more. But don't despair if your cholesterol rises or your HDL drops, for a more important measure is the ratio between the two.

Divide your TC by your HDL to get what we call the Coronary Artery Disease Risk Factor 1, known as CADRF1 for short. (If, for example, your TC is 150 and your HDL is 50, your CADRF1 is 3.0.) The lower the result, the better.

Men have an average risk of a heart attack when their CADRF1 is 4.97. That risk drops to one-half of average when the CADRF1 falls to 3.43, and continues falling as your ratio drops. But beware of an elevated CADRF1, for the risk of suffering a heart attack becomes double the average when the CADRF1 rises to 9.55.

For women, a CADRF1 of 4.44 represents an average risk of having a heart attack. The risk is cut in half when the CADRF1 falls to 3.27 (but doubles when the figure rises to 7.05).

Although not discussed in this study, other researchers have reported that Chitosan can lower the bad LDL cholesterol,[10] even as it pushes down the total cholesterol and raises the beneficial HDL. LDL (low-density lipoprotein) is believed to be, in many ways, the opposite of HDL. Where the good HDL carries cholesterol away from the artery walls, LDL is guilty of sticking it there in the first place, encouraging the formation of blockages and clots that can spell disaster. Keeping the LDL low is vital—I tell my patients that it should be 100 or less and the HDL should be above 50.

Having spent over 40 years on the front lines of crisis medicine, I've treated thousands of patients suffering from heart disease and other ailments related to elevated cholesterol. I'm delighted to report that Chitosan can help people keep their arteries, especially the vital coronary arteries, cleaner by lowering cholesterol levels.

Some people have questioned Chitosan's usefulness, pointing out that in some people it may only push the cholesterol down or increase the good HDL cholesterol by a few points. Fortunately, a few points can make a big difference. For example, every time your total cholesterol drops 1 percent, your risk of a heart attack drops by 2 percent. This means that when your total cholesterol falls by 5 points, your risk of a heart attack is automatically 10 percent lower—and that's pretty significant. Let's look at one case study.

I hadn't seen John, a 60-year-old businessman, since he'd moved away 10 years before. Then one day he returned to my office to tell me that his cholesterol was high. "My doctor did a duplex ultrasound of my neck. It showed that my neck arteries are narrowing, and I'm more likely to have a stroke. He's got me on all kinds of medicines to lower it, but they're not lowering anything except my health. The medicines have made me tired and nauseated, and my liver is sick."

John's total cholesterol was 247, which is way above the ideal of 160 (100 plus his age). His LDL was also elevated at 170, at least 70 points too high. Meanwhile, his HDL was very low at 25. It should have been 50 or more. (The National Cholesterol

Education Program states that an HDL of 35 or less should be considered an independent risk factor for coronary artery disease. I like to see my patients' HDLs at 50 or more. By either standard, John's HDL of 25 was clearly a danger sign.) These figures suggested that serious trouble lay ahead.

When I told John about Chitosan, he asked to start right away, even though his weight was not a big problem. He began by taking 1 gram before lunch and another gram before dinner. Four months later we rechecked his cholesterol. The results were gratifying.

	Before Chitosan	After Chitosan
Total cholesterol	247	195
LDL cholesterol	150	120
HDL cholesterol	25	50

Although his blood profile was not yet ideal, the Chitosan had helped him take giant strides in the right direction. You can see how well it worked by comparing his before and after CADRF1 ratios:

Before: CADRF1 = 247/25 = 9.9
This puts him at great risk of heart disease.

After: CADRF1 = 195/50 = 3.9.
He already has less than one half the standard risk of suffering from heart disease. The lower the CADRF1 continues to drop, the better.

John was overjoyed at his new numbers. He promised me, "Doc, I'll never let these numbers rise again."

Chitosan's health-saving abilities were further documented six months later when another ultrasound of John's neck showed less narrowing in his arteries. In other words, Chitosan helped widen the highway to his brain, markedly reducing his risk of a stroke. When fat gets pulled out of the plaque, the body is better able to dilate those arteries, which also widens the highway.

Is Chitosan Safe?

Chitosan *does not* interact with the body in a dangerous manner, and it *does not* add any calories or otherwise leave behind a mark. None of my patients have had any difficulty, large or small, with the substance. My findings are backed up by animal studies which have shown that "the toxicity of Chitosan is approximately equivalent to table sugar or salt."[11] In other words, you would have to ingest tremendous amounts of Chitosan before you had any difficulties.

CAUTION: However, if you are allergic to shellfish, are pregnant or breast feeding, or are under the age of 14, it's best to seek advice from your physician before

A Problem Solved

Some researchers have correctly pointed out that by pulling fatty acids from the body, Chitosan prevents us from using nutrients such as vitamins A, D, and E that are in those fats. Thus, it is theoretically possible for Chitosan to cause a nutrient deficiency.

I haven't found this to be a problem for my patients. The average person gets 40 percent of his or her calories from fat. This is more than enough; the body only needs to absorb about 6 percent fat in order to take in all the essential fatty acids and nutrients it needs.

Still, my 8-Point Fat Blocker Program successfully deals with this potential problem by including generous amounts of these nutrients in supplement form in the daily regimen, scheduled so that they're safely digested before Chitosan enters your stomach.

trying Chitosan. Also, discuss the use of Chitosan with your physician before using it if you are taking any medicines, whether prescription or nonprescription, or have any diseases or ailments. As a general rule, it is best to consult your doctor before starting any diet program.

Is Chitosan Too Good to Be True?

Not according to the studies, to my clinical experience, and the experience of countless, delighted dieters. Here is a summary of the dietary facts:

+ Chitosan is a completely natural fiber derived from the shells of shrimp and other crustaceans.

+ Chitosan acts like a magnet, its positive charge attracting and holding onto negatively charged fat from the food you just ate.

+ The indigestible Chitosan/fat gel passes through the intestines and is eliminated from the body.

+ By pulling fats and bile acids out of the body, Chitosan also helps to reduce your blood fats, total cholesterol, and bad LDL cholesterol, while increasing the good HDL cholesterol that can protect against heart disease.

+ Chitosan has been tested and found to be safe and effective in scientific studies.

By taking Chitosan before a meal, you can block the absorption of at least 3—and up to 6—grams of saturated fat for every gram of Chitosan consumed. I've been using it as part of my Fat Blocker Program for years. When combined with a healthful diet and a program of regular exercise, Chitosan is a safe and effective key to opening the door to successful dieting. You can immediately and easily cut back on your fat intake without drastically changing your diet, thanks to Chitosan, the fat magnet. Even better, you can use Chitosan as part of the Fat Blocker

Program to lose weight, improve your health, and maintain life-long eating and lifestyle habits that will keep you in vibrant health. Chitosan is found under a number of brand names in health food stores.

4

Dr. Fox's 8-Point Fat Blocker Program

Winter's snow has barely melted, and we've already begun to think of summer with mixed anticipation and dread. Sweaters and heavy clothes will soon be shed to reveal the pounds that have been put on since last bikini season. During these early months of the new year, many people begin to dust off their diet books or scan the newspaper ads for the latest wonder diet. Thus begins the latest round in the diet derby, a brutal pastime in which there are no winners.

Dana B. is typical of those who race through the diet derby, unknowingly courting disaster. This attractive, 36-year-old banker came to my office saying, "If you examine me and write a letter that says I'm healthy, I can go on this special fast that guarantees that I'll lose 20 pounds in 3 weeks."

This didn't particularly surprise me. I knew that she probably *could* lose 20 pounds in 3 weeks on a fast. I've seen people lose lots of weight quickly on various diets. I've also seen people lose their health, just as quickly, on some of these crazy diets because they're nutritionally unbalanced and they force the dieter to drop the pounds too quickly. (Simply losing too much too fast can be deadly.) And even if these diets weren't health-threatening, the fast weight loss and subsequent weight gain that they cause can result in saggy, drooping skin.

For Dana and many others, the diet derby is a way of life, unfortunately. Come March or April, they eagerly try the latest miracle diet, not really understanding the possible health consequences. But sensible eating *should* be a way of life. Dieting as an annual knock-'em-down ritual is uncomfortable, unhealthy, and unproductive. Consequently, our permanent diets should consist of the food we eat every day of the year, not the food we forgo. Our diets should also include a reasonable amount of exercise and lifestyle habits that are sensible and easy to stick to. I tell my patients that diets should be considered everyday blueprints for health.

The problem is that if looking slim and healthy while wearing nothing but a bikini, shades, and sunscreen only required a fairly easy regimen of moderate, nutritional eating coupled with a doable amount of exercise and a positive mental attitude, we would all look like movie stars. But, of course, we all know that life is not like that. If you see those stars in real life, you would see that not even they look like movie stars! Sensible eating and reasonable exercise are essential to looking good and feeling healthy. But, unfortunately, that's often not enough. Even if we are reasonable, many of us still tend to gain an unhealthy amount of body fat as we age.

The reason is, of course, that there is more to losing weight than merely eating less. While no weight-loss program is likely to succeed if caloric intake is not reduced, it does not follow that such a reduction inevitably causes weight loss. This is because our bodies are remarkably adaptable. If less food is taken in, the body recognizes this and quickly reorders its behavior: It starts to use less energy and to metabolize the food more efficiently, thus spending fewer calories. After several days of a reduced calorie diet, most people report that their rate of weight loss slows severely or stops.

The traditional way to overcome this problem—the way virtually every diet book and doctor recommends—is to step up the amount of exercise. That has the dual advantage of using up more calories as the fuel for the exercise, and of fooling the body into maintaining its metabolic rate because it believes that it cannot afford to reduce its energy output. Obviously, if the metabolism keeps operating at full tilt, exercise burns up more calories, and caloric intake is reduced, then weight loss is inevitable.

The only trouble is that this is theory, not practice. In practice what happens is that the slowdown in food intake causes the body to want to reduce the amount of energy it puts out. So, in order to conserve energy, our clever bodies command our brains to *reduce* the amount of exercise we do. That is why when we do go on a diet, one common reaction is that we don't feel like exercising.

To some extent, of course, we can overcome that tendency to avoid exercise. After all, we are gifted with free will. Our brains are capable of being strong disciplinarians. But now we are being asked to fight on two fronts at the same time: We should eat less food than our bodies are programmed to crave and exercise more at just the time when our bodies figure they should be conserving energy. In the vast majority of cases, our brains can only hold out for a while. Sooner or later, and usually sooner, we drop off our diet, ignore some or all of our exercise program, and quickly regain the weight we lost.

That's when, often in desperation, we turn to the fad diets. We cannot keep up a draconian regimen of never eating enough and always wearing ourselves out with exercise. When we are merely sensible, we gain weight. So we make the extra effort of going on a crash diet in the hope that that will solve our problem.

But the odds are stacked against us. So, what actually happens is that our weight loss is strictly temporary, and we risk our health as we waste our time, money, energy, and well-being on the diet derby.

However, things are very different with Chitosan. At last our brains have a way of outsmarting our bodies. You see, in the Chitosan program, we eat just as much as before, and as it should, our serotonin kicks in to cause us to stop eating once we are full. There is no fooling Mother Nature here. The big difference is that although we have eaten

as much as before, we don't digest and absorb as much fat. Conse-
quently, even though we have cut down on our calories, there is no
message to the body to slow down. It feels no need to conserve energy.
The happy result is that, with fewer calories being assimilated and the
same amount of energy being expended, weight loss is inevitable.

Ideally, the eating and exercise habits that we form in our early
years and carry into adulthood will ensure that we stay slim and
healthy for a lifetime. But, of course they don't—and for a very
good reason. When we are young, we tend to be very active. We
eat a lot, but we burn off a lot of calories too. Then, as we get
older, the eating habits remain but a slower pace takes over and
we move a little less. We tend to think before we act (which is
often a very good thing, but tends to burn up fewer calories!).
We get married and settle down, which sometimes involves
eating more between meals and exercising less. We become
more affluent and drive cars or take taxis instead of peddling
our bikes or running for a bus. All in all, we eat as much or
more, but we use up less of the food we eat. Instead, we store
the food in the form of fat. Our bodies are waiting for that rainy
day when the food runs out. But, of course, that day never
comes. McDonald's keeps serving. And the fat stays on.

Moreover, we are human and sometimes do unwise things—
like eating huge Thanksgiving dinners (and then gorging on the
leftover stuffing for the next three days!).

So, gradually, we gain weight, and suddenly we realize we
are at risk both physically and in our jobs and personal relations.
We have gone from slim to pudgy, and from pudgy to overweight. Almost overnight, it seems, we are fat.

In such situations, we sometimes find ourselves in need of
losing a considerable amount of weight at an accelerated pace.
In that case, Chitosan may not be enough; just cutting out, say,
15 grams of fat twice a day (or about 270 calories) may not be
enough to achieve the results you want. While you will lose
weight, you may not do so fast enough to meet your needs.

Similarly, if you are gaining weight, just adding Chitosan
will slow down or even stop the weight gain, but it may not be

sufficient to reverse it and make you lose weight. In that case, you will have to do more. But remember, with Chitosan you are already a good part of the way there. If you cut out 10, 15, 20, even 25 grams of fat a day without *any* effort, it will require only a relatively small effort to cut down on the additional calories in order to really start losing weight. There will be no need to try extreme diets you cannot stick to. Instead, you will be able to make reasonable, sustainable adjustments to your eating habits.

So, if you should find yourself in that situation, do yourself a favor and adopt these weight-loss philosophies:

1. Good nutrition and weight loss must go hand in hand.
2. The use of nutrients can help bolster your health.
3. Exercise is diet's natural partner.
4. Success begins with belief.
5. Thin shouldn't be confused with healthy.
6. Avoid fad diets.
7. Be reasonable. No one succeeds in losing weight by starting a program they cannot reasonably sustain.
8. Use Chitosan. It will help you achieve your weight-loss goals.

1. *Good nutrition and weight loss must go hand in hand.* The quickest, simplest way to lose weight is to stop eating altogether. It's called starvation, and it's *very* bad for your health because it causes the body to turn on itself and consume its own tissues for energy. Even short fasts can be dangerous for some people. Whether dieting or not, your body depends upon a steady supply of protein, carbohydrate, fat, vitamins, minerals, and water. So, if you want to lose carefully but relatively quickly, you must ensure that you're getting an adequate amount of the nutrients that your body needs. For this reason, a large part of your diet should consist of complex carbohydrates in the form of fresh vegetables, fruits, and whole grains. These foods should be supplemented with reasonable amounts of meat, poultry, fish, or cooked dried beans and low-fat or nonfat dairy products. But, unlike your previous attempts, you don't have to cut out all red

meat, give up butter entirely, or never eat a cookie again. The extra fat those treats bring with them is taken care of by the Chitosan.

Vegetables and fruits are full of the complex carbohydrates needed for energy, vitamins, and minerals. Yet (apart from olives and avocados) they contain very little fat. Unfortunately, most of us don't get anywhere near the recommended amount of these two delicious groups of foods, which is why I suggest to my patients (even those who are *not* trying to lose weight) that they carry a plastic bag full of fresh vegetables and fruits with them every day. My theory is, if you have it in front of you, you'll eat it!

Fill your Chitosan bag with raw lettuce, broccoli, celery, parsley, snow peas, carrots, and other green vegetables. A second bag can be used for fresh fruits such as apples, peaches, oranges, or anything else that's in season. Put your bags in your briefcase, lunch pail, desk, or car—wherever they'll be handy—and munch on the vegetables during the day. Carrying these bags can help you lose weight by constantly reminding you of your goal while giving you a nutritious, low-calorie alternative to fattening foods. Nibbling from your Chitosan bags also takes the sharp edge off your appetite, so you won't be ravenously hungry and likely to overeat.

In fact, in many of my patients, I have found that just this simple trick coupled with Chitosan is all it takes for them to lose weight. At the very least, eating extra fruits and vegetables—and reminding yourself to do so in this way—means that you won't be tempted to eat more just because the Chitosan lets you do so. It's obvious that if you take Chitosan to block the fat, but then eat a whole lot more, you will not lose weight. But we are strange creatures, and sometimes we have to remind ourselves of the obvious!

Remember that a slow, steady weight loss is much healthier than sudden drops. Always keep in mind that your overall state of nutrition and health is what's important—if everything else is in good shape, adding Chitosan will take care of your weight problem. But if you are seriously overeating, Chitosan will only go part of the way; you also have to make other adjustments to your eating and lifestyle habits. If you do, I can assure you that your body will find its optimal weight.

2. *The use of nutrients can help bolster your health.* Ideally, we would always get all vitamins, minerals, and other nutrients that we need from our foods. Unfortunately, the way our foods are grown, shipped, stored, and processed can rob them of vital nutrients. That is one reason I generally recommend that my patients take good amounts of four supplements that I call the 4 ACES. They include

A—alpha carotene, beta carotene, and other carotenoids
C—vitamin C
E—vitamin E
S—the mineral selenium

The 4 ACES are powerful antioxidants that help slow the onset of the signs of aging, while helping to protect against heart disease and cancer. Coenzyme Q10, alpha lipotene, and pycnogenol are also very helpful for their antioxidant and free-radical quenching properties.

I generally recommend that my patients take a supplement that contains alpha carotene, beta carotene, luetin, lycopene, zeaxanthin, and cryptoxanthin. All these are available in a single tablet. Just take one in the morning, one at night. In addition, I suggest 500–1000 mg. of vitamin C twice a day to start, 400 I.U. of vitamin E in the form of d-alpha tocopherol twice a day, and 200 mcg. of selenium once a day. Take half the supplements with your morning meal, the other half before going to bed. If you take them around lunch or dinnertime (the same times you'll be taking Chitosan) they may not all be absorbed into your body. That is because some vitamins, such as vitamins A, D, and E are fat soluble, and since the Chitosan removes a good amount of the fat you eat, it could theoretically remove the vitamins dissolved in it. This has never been a problem for my patients, but it's a good idea to talk it over with your physician, and if there is any concern, take your supplements several hours before or after the time you plan to take your Chitosan.

3. *Exercise is diet's natural partner.* Steady aerobic exercise (jogging, brisk walking, bicycling, swimming, aerobic dancing, etc.) will raise your metabolic rate, thus helping you to burn more calories throughout the day. Wogging (alternating walking and jogging) is an easy way to exercise. The ideal amount of exercise for most people is 30–45 minutes a day, 4–5 times a week. This may seem like an ambitious goal at first. So, rather than set yourself a task you can't stick to in the long run, I suggest you set a more limited goal: Simply promise yourself that you will do a little more exercise tomorrow than you did today.

With Chitosan, you are already cutting down on your fat and calorie intake so the tendency to lose weight already exists. But you don't want to negate that tendency by allowing yourself to slow down. Rather, by adding just a little more exercise, you will be sure the program is fully effective.

So, if you usually do no exercise at all, I suggest you start by walking a hundred yards. The next day, make it a hundred yards and a flight of stairs (get off the elevator one story below your office and walk up). Of course, if you are already doing 25 minutes of hard running, then moving up to 30 minutes is just right!

4. *Success begins with belief.* As Frank Lloyd Wright said, "The thing always happens that you believe in. And the belief in a thing makes it happen." Begin your Fat Blocker Program by visualizing yourself as the trim, healthy person you want to be. With your mind's eye, picture yourself at your desired weight, perhaps standing by a pool. Don't stop there; see yourself slim during the holiday season as well—slim the year round. I teach my patients to see it, then say it, and above all *feel* it. Affirm that you are what you want to be: "I am slim and healthy." Say this out loud and repeat it often, it works better. So, try saying it out loud, 50 times a day. As my friend Reverend Ike says, "Positive affirmations are seeing and feeling yourself—in your mind— already being, doing, and having what you want." Having dealt with countless dieting patients I can confidently report that the belief in your ability to control your body and to be slim and

healthy is a vital part of dieting—and of life. One of the main advantages of Chitosan, and one not written about very often, is that it will greatly strengthen your conviction that you will lose weight. And, no wonder, for the product obviously works. At last, you can really believe you will be able to lose weight. How can you believe in other diets that you have tried over and over without success? But now, with Chitosan, you will be able to believe. And all things are possible to those who believe.

5. *Thin shouldn't be confused with healthy.* I treat many very thin models—women who weigh between 95 and 110 pounds. They're thin, but at the same time some of them are significantly "overfat!" Of course you'd never know it by looking at them. Still, body weight is accounted for by a combination of lean body tissue (bones and muscle) and fat tissue. It's quite possible for a 100-pound woman to look slim but carry only 70 of those pounds as lean body tissue and 30 of them as fat. But fat should account for no more than 20 to 25 percent of a healthy woman's body weight, and about 15 percent of the average man's weight. So the 100-pound woman in our example is overfat and therefore unhealthy. It's much more prudent to focus on improving your health rather than on trying to reach a designated dress size or number on the scale. Remember: Thinness and good health are two different things.

◆

Unhealthy Eating Practices That Can Be Brought on by Dieting

Compulsive Eating—The compulsive eater is obsessed with eating; extrasensitive to the sight, smell, and thought of food; chronically worried about his or her appearance; likely to rank everyone he or she sees on a thin-to-fat scale; thinking constantly about the next meal.

Anorexia—Anorexics impose on themselves a severe, unhealthy restriction of eating; are consumed with thoughts of food; impose and adhere to rigorous exercise regimens; don't believe they are thin even though they may have lost more than one-fifth of their body weight; seek to control their emotions through self-starvation.

Bulimia—The bulimic eats voraciously (binges) then purges (vomits, starves, or takes laxatives, and/or engages in extreme amounts of exercise) as a means of weight control; has an insatiable desire to eat and finally gives in to it, allowing the appetite unrestrained expression. Then, fear of weight gain causes the victim to purge. This binging-and-purging cycle can occupy most of the victim's time, occurring as many as 10–20 times a day.

Oral Expulsion Syndrome—Victims of this syndrome chew food but spit it out rather than swallow it. Some may spend hours chewing in secret, and can develop intense anxiety about swallowing. They may become seriously malnourished, isolated, and fearful.

---

6. *Avoid fad diets.* In the early 1980s I treated many people who had lost weight (as well as their health) on dangerous fad diets. Some had even used cocaine to slim their bodies. (It does work, but its effects on health are disastrous.) As you'll see in Chapter 11, most fad diets are useless, and many are harmful. Moreover, with Chitosan, they are unnecessary. Now there is an alternative that is realistic, one that truly works.

7. *Be reasonable.* We were all born with different bodies. Most of us will never be fashion-model slim, and we can ruin our health trying to be. Even with the regular ingestion of Chitosan, we may not achieve what we desire if that desire is unreasonable. For our bodies are wondrous machines that struggle against being abused.

So, unlike everything you have tried or heard before, I say be very careful when it comes to restricting your eating too much. It's not good for you, and it won't work. Don't get me wrong—I'm all for avoiding the pitfalls of obesity. I believe that maintaining a normal weight is crucial to good health. Still, I tell my patients that I'd rather see them carry a few extra pounds than resort to starving themselves or engaging in unhealthy eating practices. Up to now, this has been something of a dilemma: You want to control what you're eating to some degree (by staying away from too much fat, sugar, salt; eating more vegetables and fruits; etc.) yet you don't want to over control and wind up with a diet you cannot live with, or even with an eating disorder. So how can you walk the line?

Well, in addition to Chitosan, which is obviously your first line of defense, here are a number of other reasonable strategies.

First, only eat when you're hungry. In particular, if you feel hungry between regular scheduled mealtimes, make sure it's truly hunger that you feel—not boredom, a twinge in your stomach, or an unmet emotional need. When you first feel that you're hungry between meals, wait ten minutes. Many times we confuse a brief pang with true hunger. If you're still hungry ten minutes later, munch a little from your Chitosan bag. Then, if you're still hungry or if you truly crave an occasional high-fat treat, take your Chitosan and eat it! Always listen to your body's signals. If you're especially hungry one day, go ahead and eat larger portions.

The same principle applies to your meals. By using your secret weapon when you need it, you can afford to eat that extra portion you really want. That way, you'll be able to stay with a healthful eating program. On the other hand, if you're not very hungry one day, eat smaller portions of lighter foods. But do make sure you always get the minimum recommended number of servings each day. You *must* have your three meals and two snacks, even if you're not feeling very hungry and they are quite small. By all means, take smaller portions if that's appropriate, but do eat. Your body needs the nutrients.

Second, realize that weight loss is not a race—the point is to keep moving in the direction of your ideal body weight. Even if you feel the urgent need to lose weight quickly, there is only so much you can do. And slowly losing weight is much better for your health. Your body is more likely to adjust to the new weight and you're more likely to adopt gradually but permanently the new eating habits so that your weight will continue to decline until it gets to your ideal weight. That's where it will stabilize. As long as you keep taking your Chitosan—and a little extra if you occasionally overindulge—there is no need to regain the weight you have lost—ever.

Eating disorders are, of course, a curse that comes with too much emphasis on losing weight fast, too many crash diets, and too much worship at the altar of unnecessary thinness. At their worst, true eating disorders destroy healthy living and can even lead to death. But they usually begin gradually, and the best time to deal with them is when they are just starting.

The question is, how will you know if you're beginning to develop some unhealthy eating practices? To provide you with the answer, try this Eating Disorders Questionnaire:

◆

Eating Disorders Questionnaire

Put a check (√) by any of the items that apply to you.

_____ 1. My friends tell me that I'm thin but I don't believe them because I feel fat.

_____ 2. I frequently eat when I'm not hungry.

_____ 3. I have had an out-of-control eating binge in the past year.

_____ 4. Food is usually the first thing I think of when I wake up in the morning.

_____ 5. I seem to be constantly on a diet.

_____ 6. I have become obsessed with food to the point that I cannot go through a day without worrying about what I will or will not eat.

_____ 7. I have dieted to an abnormally low weight because it makes me feel that I'm in control.

_____ 8. My menstrual periods have stopped or become irregular for no known medical reason.

_____ 9. I frequently eat to the point of being uncomfortably full.

_____ 10. I panic if I cannot exercise to compensate for food I have eaten or plan to eat.

_____ 11. After a binge, I have done at least one of the following in the past year: forced myself to vomit; used laxatives, enemas, or colonics; fasted; exercised in an unusually vigorous way.

_____ 12. I would be very upset if I got on the scale tomorrow and found that I had gained two pounds.

_____ 13. I play with the food on my plate so people will think I have eaten more than I really have.

_____ 14. I feel uneasy about eating in general.

_____ 15. I often eat to make myself feel better emotionally, and afterward I feel guilty about it.

_____ 16. I restrict my eating in public and then binge secretly in private.

_____ 17. I use laxatives, enemas, or colonics at least twice weekly.

_____ 18. I find myself talking at length about food, weight, recipes, restaurants, diets, and other food-related topics.

_____ 19. People around me seem very interested in what I do or don't eat and I get angry at them for pushing food on me.

If you've checked off more than 2 items, you may have a problem with your eating. Checking even one item can be a sign of danger. In addition, if you or others in your immediate family have had an alcohol or drug abuse problem, this may predispose you to developing an eating disorder. Obviously, it doesn't mean you have one, but should warn you to beware of the possibility. In any case, if you are in any doubt, or see any danger signs, see your physician or registered dietitian, and take this questionnaire with you.

◆

8. *Use Chitosan. It will help you achieve your weight-loss goals.* This simple statement is the most important weight-loss information you may ever receive. It is at the heart of the only weight-loss program that seems to work for everybody, every time. Because Chitosan is such an effective fat-blocking agent, as part of a complete, easy-to-follow dietary and health regimen, it serves as the

key to unlocking good health and weight loss. Take *at least* 1 gram of Chitosan half an hour before lunch, and at least another 1 gram half an hour before dinner, and you will see a permanent improvement in your weight. Taking Chitosan half an hour *before* meals is best, although it can still be taken up to half an hour after. Of course, you can take up to 4 or 5 grams of Chitosan and your weight loss will be greater. But remember, you should not exceed the recommended label dosage. In any case, keep eating sensibly, exercise reasonably, and keep taking Chitosan routinely, and you will be healthier, lighter, and probably a great deal happier!

5

◆

Putting the Fat Blocker Program into Practice, and Why

Before starting the Fat Blocker Program, read this book in its entirety and consult your physician. Then weigh yourself. Write down your actual weight and your target weight. (Use the height-weight table in Chapter 2 to find your ideal weight.)

Actual Weight _____   Ideal Weight _____

Now call your physician and ask for the results of your latest blood test. Specifically, you want to know your total cholesterol, HDL, LDL, VLDL, and triglyceride (blood fat) levels. If they are not available, or are more than a year old, arrange to have another test as soon as possible. Write your results below in the left column. Ideal levels are listed in the right column.

Actual total
cholesterol _____

Ideal cholesterol: 100 plus your age

Actual HDL _____

Ideal HDL: 50 or more

Actual LDL _____

Ideal LDL: less than 100

Actual VLDL _____

Ideal VLDL: less than 20

Actual triglycerides _____

Ideal triglycerides: less than 100

Now that you know where you are and where you want to be, tailor eating and exercise programs that meet your own personal needs by following the guidelines in this book. They are simple not only to understand but to stick to, because Chitosan makes a gentle, nonrigorous, weight-loss program as effective as a tough, almost impossible one. Here are the steps to take to follow my program:

1) *Design your eating program*—You should begin by following Plan I, which gives the minimum amount of servings from each food group. If you find that you're just too hungry, add an extra serving of one or more food groups. Don't try to cut down too much. If you're hungry all the time, you won't stick to your diet. So, just cut down a little bit. However, do remember not to exceed the maximum amount of servings. You'll have the most leeway in the grain group (between 6 to 11 servings a day) and the least in the extra group (which should be limited as much as possible). Naturally, the more servings you add, the slower your weight loss will be. However, it's better to eat enough to feel comfortably full, than to feel constantly hungry and then inevitably binge.

2) *Take your other supplements as necessary*—To ensure that the Chitosan does not interfere with the absorption of any fat-soluble nutrients, take half of them with breakfast (when you do not take Chitosan), and the other half before going to bed (several hours after your dose of Chitosan). Discuss your supplement needs with your physician.

3) *Design your exercise program*—If you're over 40 or you have any illnesses or ailments, see your physician first. Look for an exercise that's enjoyable; you're more likely to stick with it. Be sure to stretch and warm up appropriately, and never overdo it.

Let me repeat that. It's just as important as a sensible, unthreatening eating program. Don't try to do more exercise than you enjoy and can keep doing. If you start by moving from essentially no exercise to a daily regimen of an hour of heavy aerobics, you'll exhaust yourself, probably feel nauseous, and quit. If you overstrain your body, it will rebel. Pain, tiredness, excessive panting, overheating, heart palpitations—none of these symptoms of overexertion are good for you, and your body knows it. In reaction, it forces you to slow down, and it sends ever more urgent messages to your brain to tell you to stop being so foolish.

Rather, start your exercise program slowly by adding just a little more to what you are currently doing. Try to make it fun. And always keep this goal in mind when you're exercising: You want to burn calories, increase your metabolic rate, and improve your health, not set Olympic records.

4) *Take in the right amount of Chitosan*—As you move to a reasonable diet (i.e., less than you are now eating) and a reasonable exercise program (i.e., just slightly more than you are now doing), you will be reducing your calorie intake a little and increasing your calorie burn rate by a small amount. Alone, these minor improvements would make little difference. But now you are adding Chitosan to the mix, and thus losing a significant proportion of the fat you ingest. And that will make a big difference.

The key here is to tailor the amount of Chitosan you take to the amount of fat you consume. (The table on page 45 will let you decide on what is right for you.)

But there is even more to this approach. For, over time, another tremendously important benefit starts to appear. As your slight decrease in eating and your slight increase in exercise start to work together with the Chitosan to lower your weight, you will find that your energy starts to increase. Without even thinking about it, you will find yourself increasing your exercise. At the same time, because you are more active and less of a couch potato, you will find yourself snacking less. Gradually, what started out as a very mild exercise program will transform itself into a much more vigorous one—more than you could possibly have managed. In fact, you may even find that you can cut down on the amount of Chitosan you need to consume. Without really noticing it, you've formed new habits and patterns of eating and exercising.

After some time following the precepts of the Fat Blocker Eating Program and the Fat Blocker Exercise Program, you will find that you have created the foundation for a lifetime of excellent health. You will have developed a recipe for permanent weight control that is more precious than the finest gems. In your previous attempts (if you are like most people), you eventually allowed yourself to slip back into old habits and lose all of the progress that you had made. But now things are different. With Chitosan, you can maintain your slim, attractive body indefinitely. If you do indulge in the occasional splurge, take some extra Chitosan. The rest of the time, take only the amount of Chitosan you need to keep your fat intake under control.

Scientific Proof That the Fat Blocker Program Works

I've had a great many positive experiences treating patients with the program I describe in this book. But even the most exciting clinical experience is stronger if it's backed up by scientific studies. Let's take a look at just a few of the many studies showing how fat reduction and the other elements included in my program reduce the risk of heart disease, stroke, cancer, diabetes, gallstones, kidney stones, hypertension, arthritis, and ulcers.

THE FAT BLOCKER PROGRAM GUARDS AGAINST HEART DISEASE AND STROKE

Most of what we call heart disease is really coronary artery disease, or clogged arteries. The tiny coronary arteries supplying fresh blood to the heart muscle become blocked by plugs made of cholesterol, fat, and debris. As a result, some part of the heart dies. If the blockage is severe enough, the entire heart (and the person it keeps alive) will die. A very similar process can happen in the arteries carrying fresh blood to the brain, leading to a stroke (a brain attack).

Clearly, keeping the arteries clean is vital—and the Fat Blocker Program can help do just that. Switching overweight people from a standard high-fat diet to a low-fat, low-calorie diet almost always reduces their levels of total cholesterol as well as the LDL bad cholesterol[1]—provided, obviously, that they stay with it. But obese people usually got that way because they love to eat and don't love to exercise. To ask them to stay with any truly tough diet indefinitely is unrealistic. That is why, up to now, there has been no surely effective, permanent way to help people lose weight. The statistics prove the point: Individually and collectively we are gaining weight. And the personal experience of virtually every overweight person attests to it: "I just can't lose weight and keep it off."

But now, with Chitosan, that is all different. My patients who use Chitosan can lose the fat that is putting their arteries at risk—and considerably extend their life expectancy. And they can do so permanently, and without having to resort to an eating program that is harsh enough to harm the quality of their lives. Overweight people (like almost everyone) love food—they just don't like the excess weight it brings with it. Now, with Chitosan, they can enjoy reasonable amounts of what they love—and not have to put up with the weight they hate.

Many patients who come to see me are still gaining weight. And there is no doubt that is very dangerous. For example, a 1990 study appearing in the *Journal of the American Medical Association*[2] reported that as the consumption of fat increased, so did the risk of new lesions. (Lesions are wounds in the arteries where cholesterol-fat plugs can take root and grow.) Yet, to ask many of these people to stop gaining weight by eating much less is like asking the tide not to rise. On the other hand, it is easy for my patients to consume Chitosan, and that, coupled with *some* reduction in their food intake, is almost always enough to stop further weight gain.

As for strokes, we've known for some time that the risk of

this disease is greater in areas where people eat a higher-fat diet, such as the "stroke belt" in the southern United States, where fried chicken and the like is a universal delicacy. On the other hand, in geographic areas where people eat more fresh vegetables and fruits, the incidence of stroke tends to be lower.[3] This was confirmed by a study appearing in the *New England Journal of Medicine*.[4] The 12-year-long study involving 859 men and women ages 50–79 found that eating more vegetables and fruits could help to reduce the risk of stroke. Thus, by combining Chitosan with more vegetables and fruits, the Fat Blocker Program helps to reduce your risk of stroke two ways: by lowering fat and hence the bad cholesterol and by raising good cholesterol.

THE FAT BLOCKER PROGRAM REDUCES
THE RISK OF CANCER

Way back in the 1940s, medical researchers realized that obesity and cancer were linked: Being obese increased both the risk of developing cancer and the speed with which malignancies progressed.[5] Since then, numerous studies have shown that you have a reduced risk of getting cancer if you eat a low-fat, low-cholesterol, moderate-protein, high-fiber diet. You can achieve the same objective by including Chitosan in a moderate-fat, moderate-cholesterol diet, which for many is a more practical way of attacking the problem. Here's how:

✦ **Excess Fat Encourages Cancer**—Researchers studying dietary patterns of several hundred Swedes found that high-fat diets were linked to urothelial (kidney and bladder) cancer.[6] Eating a diet high in saturated fat was linked to an increased risk of lung and prostate cancer in a case-controlled study involving members of five different ethnic groups.[7] Fried foods are especially dangerous. A 1985 report in the *Journal of the American Medical Association*[8] describes a study involving over 16,000 Seventh Day Adventist women. Those who ate three or more eggs per week were three times more likely to develop fatal ovarian cancer than those who consumed fewer eggs. Eating fried fish, chicken, and potatoes was also a risk factor for the disease. Of course, I urge my patients to eat less of this terribly fatty type of food. And certainly they can follow my advice up to a point. Beyond that, many rely on Chitosan to cut down their fat intake. And, since the fat absorbed by the Chitosan will have the same effect as fat not eaten in the first place, the health benefits are identical.

✦ **Fiber Guards Against Cancer**—Chitosan is a dietary fiber. Thus, in addition to its remarkable fat-blocking characteristics, it also gives consumers the benefit that high-fiber products of any sort bring. Thus, while its ability to cut down on the excess fat that is associated with increased cancer risk is determinant in the decision to use Chitosan, its characteristics as a fiber further help to guard against various forms of the killer. High-fiber diets have been found to lower the risk of developing cancers of the breast,[9] colon and rectum,[10] pancreas,[11] and prostate.[12]

THE FAT BLOCKER PROGRAM REDUCES THE RISK OF DIABETES

The onset of Type II diabetes mellitus is often associated with weight gain. That's why losing weight via reduced fat intake (achieved by trying to eat less fat and taking Chitosan to remove a lot of fat we do eat) is often the "medicine" of choice for this disease. I've had a great deal of success with my Type II diabetic patients by just getting them to slim down with Chitosan and a healthier diet. The studies in the scientific literature back up my experiences.

Way back in 1927, Dr. Joslin, founder of the famous Joslin Clinic, wrote in the *Journal of the American Medical Association,* "With an excess of fat, diabetes begins; and from an excess of fat, diabetics die . . ."[13] Today we know that the high-fat diet can make us less responsive to our own insulin.[14] The body makes insulin to control the blood sugar. But if our body cells develop a resistance to insulin, our blood sugar levels soar and we develop diabetes. As I'm writing this, the latest issue of the *Journal of the American Medical Association* has just arrived. In it is a report titled "Dietary Fiber, Glycemic Load, and Risk of Non-Insulin-Dependent Diabetes Mellitus in Women."[15] The authors of this study report that a low-fiber diet containing high amounts of sugar increases the risk of diabetes in women. (I've found that the same is true for men.) Here are the major ways in which the Fat Blocker Program helps prevent and/or treat this problem:

+ **Losing Weight Reduces the Risk of Type II Diabetes—** According to the National Institutes of Health 1986 Consensus Development Conference,[16] nearly 80 percent of those with Type II diabetes were obese when it struck. Increased weight, being obese for long periods of time, and extra fat stored in the upper body are all factors that increase the risk of developing this disease. Thin people can also develop Type II diabetes, but are much less likely to do so than their obese counterparts.

+ **Complex Carbohydrates Guard Against Diabetes—** While fat is likely to accelerate the onset of Type II diabetes, eating a diet rich in complex carbohydrates will do the opposite. We know, for example, that diabetes is rare among African villagers who consume diets high in fiber, while it's much more common among people in more "advanced" countries (like the United States) where a low-fiber, highly processed diet is common.[17] Investigations into the way the body responds to various foods have found that diabetics do much better when they eat a high-fiber diet, especially one that includes a good amount of peas, beans, and lentils. When consuming this kind of diet, the diabetic body does a better job of controlling the blood sugar, and blood fats levels also improve.[18] Therefore, the American Diabetes Association suggests that diabetics consume generous amounts of fiber and other complex carbohydrates while reducing their intake of cholesterol and saturated fat.[19]

By including Chitosan, really the only way in which many people can lose weight successfully, while also recommending that you fill up with healthful complex carbohydrates, the Fat Blocker Program acts as both a medicine for and a preventive measure against Type II diabetes. In addition, gradually increasing the exercise component of your life helps to keep body weight down and blood pressure, cholesterol, and blood sugar under control, important factors for the prevention or treatment of this disease.

THE FAT BLOCKER PROGRAM REDUCES GALLSTONES AND KIDNEY STONES

Diet plays a distinct role in the development of gallstones, those "rocks" made primarily of cholesterol that grow in the gallbladder, causing pain, nausea, vomiting, jaundice, infections, and other problems. It's clear that high-fat, high-calorie diets that are bereft of vegetables increase the risk of developing gallstones, as do diets high in fried or other fatty foods.[20]

While fatty foods, excess calories, and a lack of vegetables are all risk factors for gallstones, that risk drops when we eat lots of fiber. The protective effects of fiber were noted as far back as 1969, with the publication of a report that compared 101 people who had gallstones to another 101 who did not. The study found that those who did not have the stones ate more vegetables and fruits, suggesting that the fiber in these foods protected against gallstones. Other investigations have confirmed these early results.[21]

The Fat Blocker Program clearly fits the requirements of an antigallstone regimen. It encourages you to eat more of the fiber-filled foods that help keep your gallbladder free of painful stones while helping you to reduce your weight. And, as a side benefit, this same regimen helps prevent the formation of kidney stones. Studies have shown that eating a high-fiber,[22] low-fat[23] diet also guards against this excruciating but common ailment.

Thus, here again Chitosan, which provides both the mechanism for reducing fat and the extra fiber that is called for, represents as close to a magic bullet as we are likely to see. Moreover, it works its magic without any of the side effects that drugs usually have.

THE FAT BLOCKER PROGRAM HELPS KEEP BLOOD PRESSURE UNDER CONTROL

Often called the silent killer because it provokes no discernable symptoms in the early stages, elevated blood pressure can be a killer. Some 60 million Americans suffer from this disease, which is more likely to strike if you are obese or eat a diet high in saturated fat and low in fiber.

We know that populations consuming large amounts of fiber do not suffer from the age-related rise in blood pressure seen among those eating low-fiber, high-fat diets. We also know that adding fiber to the diet lowers elevated blood pressure—it can even lower it in those with normal pressure readings.[24]

The *British Medical Journal*[25] reported on a study looking at the relationship between fiber and blood pressure. Ninety-four people ranging in age from 18–60 were grouped according to their fiber intake. Those who consumed high-fiber diets had lower blood pressure than those who did not. To test the immediate effect of fiber on blood pressure, 11 of those who normally ate a high-fiber diet decreased their fiber intake. Four months later, their blood pressures had increased. Meanwhile, 31 people who normally consumed low amounts of fiber began eating more fiber. Four months later, their blood pressure levels had dropped.

A study discussed in *The Lancet*,[26] a prestigious British medical journal, looked at 46 lean patients with elevated blood pressure. Some were given a fiber pill containing 7 grams of fiber while others received a placebo. Three months later, the average blood pressure had dropped significantly among those who had been taking the fiber, while it remained the same in those who had not.

It's clear that blood pressure responds to the amount of fiber we eat. As a fiber, Chitosan helps to block hypertension by encouraging blood pressure to drop down to normal levels.

THE FAT BLOCKER PROGRAM RELIEVES ARTHRITIS

More than 50 million Americans suffer from various forms of arthritis. Their joints are achy, stiff, and swollen. It hurts to move. Many of my arthritis patients were severely depressed when they first came to see me, for their joint problems often prevented them from exercising, enjoying other activities, getting through the day, or even performing routine self-care.

Many factors can prompt the onset of the various forms of arthritis, but it's clear that obesity makes things worse, especially if the arthritis affects the weight-bearing joints of the spine, hips, knees, or ankles—as it usually does. Slimming down to your ideal weight with Chitosan and my Fat Blocker Program is an excellent beginning for anyone who suffers from this disease.

In fact, switching to the Chitosan-based Fat Blocker Program aids in several ways. First, it helps you to lose weight. Second, it reduces the amount of fat that remains in your body, which can help with certain forms of the disease. For example, elevated levels of saturated fatty acids in the blood and fat tissues have been associated with rheumatoid arthritis.[27] Third, the ability to gradually increase the amount of exercise you do is an excellent medicine for many forms of the disease. Exercise helps to increase and maintain joint stability, improve joint function, and often does much to decrease pain.

THE FAT BLOCKER PROGRAM SOOTHES ULCERS

We've also known for years that eating a high-fiber, low-fat diet can reduce the risk of ulcers. While I don't recommend Chitosan as a primary treatment, I've found that taking Chitosan can ameliorate the pains of ulcers or gastritis.

In one study,[28] 38 patients with peptic ulcer disease were compared to 40 healthy controls. Those who developed the disease ate significantly less fiber than those who were ulcer-free. Another fascinating study[29] involved 73 people whose duodenal ulcers had recently healed. Thirty-eight of them were randomly chosen and asked to include lots of whole-grain bread, vegetables and porridge in their diets, while the other 35 were asked to avoid these same foods. Six months later, only 45 percent of the high-fiber group had suffered relapses, compared to 80 percent of the low-fiber eaters.

A similar study involved 42 patients with chronic duodenal ulcers. Half of them were put on a diet containing a good amount of unrefined wheat, which is high in fiber. The other 20 were asked to continue eating their low-fiber diets. Five years later, only 14 percent of the high-fiber eaters suffered relapses, compared to 81 percent of those consuming little fiber.[30]

As shown in these preliminary studies, Chitosan and the Fat Blocker Eating Program may help you prevent and/or treat ulcers.

You Can Do It!

This program has worked for many of my patients, whether they've been chubby, rotund, obese, or just plain big. It can work for you, too! The beauty of this program is that it never seems overwhelming. Unlike other weight reduction plans, I am not asking you to develop whole new eating and exercise regimens overnight. If you find that you can adopt the entire program all at once, begin simply by making a minor reduction in your fat intake. Gradually add in the other elements of the program as you feel comfortable. And remember, Chitosan can help you achieve your weight-loss goals. In no time at all, you'll find yourself on the road to losing weight and gaining health!

6

The Fat Blocker Eating Program

Ah, food! We can't live without it, but sometimes it seems like we can't live *with* it, either. It can make us fat, it can encourage cancer, it can promote heart disease. We can become obsessed with it, and yet we *have* to eat, for our bodies need a wide variety of nutrients every day in order to keep humming along in peak condition. How can we get everything we need without overdoing it? And how can we feel truly satisfied without gaining unwanted pounds?

The answer is simpler than you might think. Take a lesson from the Biblical story of Daniel. The king told his steward to feed Daniel and his three friends the richest food and the finest wine, but Daniel declined. He wanted only grains, vegetables, and water. After 10 days on this regime, Daniel appeared much healthier and better fed than his friends who had been feasting on heavier fare.

I like to remind my patients to eat like Daniel did. The bulk of the diet should be made up of grains (whole-grain breads, cereals, and pastas). To that, add plenty of vegetables (raw or lightly steamed are best) and several pieces of fruit. Then, add small amounts of meat, fish, poultry, peas, beans, or lentils for protein, plus modest amounts of dairy products for calcium.

Fatty foods like salad dressing, oil, butter, margarine, and mayonnaise should be used sparingly, just for flavor. Sweets should also be eaten only occasionally, as a treat.

Ah, you say, but Daniel was a saint. He survived the lion's den. He had courage and powers of self-control most of us lack. Maybe he could eschew the king's delectable goodies, but could the rest of us? How can we adhere to such a rigorous food plan? We may feel we *need* steaks and brownies and donuts at least occasionally for our souls if not for our bodies. That, of course, is the key point about every diet and most diet books. They all work if we are Daniellike ascetics. They don't work if we are mere earthbound mortals. At least, not until now.

Eating Should Be Fun, Too!

It's important that we watch what we consume. But it's just as important that we live life fully, enjoying eating as much as possible. Most of us can't follow a strict, stringent diet for long. We wind up frustrated, convinced that we might as well forget the whole thing. That's why we should give ourselves a break, realizing that it's natural (and even good for us) to eat "forbidden" foods now and again. I know that when I visit my hometown of South Philadelphia, I always have a Pat's Steak Sandwich and a Tastykake, a delicious chocolate cupcake I've enjoyed since I was a child. All of us have similar vices, no doubt, and if we don't indulge them, they start to dominate our thoughts. We become obsessed with them and then we *really* overindulge.

Yet, the truth is that eating high-calorie sugary foods in small amounts won't affect your health in the long run provided you don't also overindulge on a consistent basis in eating fat. The key is to eat the foods you love, cutting down on them as much as you can, while taking your Chitosan to make sure you keep your fat intake low. Since you are now eating a large proportion of what you want when you want it, your desire to splurge will be greatly reduced.

Guidelines for the Fat Blocker Eating Program

The Fat Blocker Eating Program is really not a diet. Instead, it's a guide to lifelong good eating. In fact, if every American adopted this eating plan and followed it scrupulously, the national rates of cancer, heart disease, and diabetes would come crashing down. Immune systems would get a tremendous boost, so that infections and illnesses would carry less of a punch. Everyday health problems that drain us of energy, patience, and joy, like chronic headaches, allergies, and certain skin conditions, might become things of the past. So don't think that you'll be depriving your family once you start planning your meals according to the Fat Blocker guidelines. Actually, you'll be doing them a big favor.

THE IDEALS

Before proceeding further, I want to emphasize that for much of the balance of this chapter, I shall be concentrating on what constitutes an ideal diet. If you stuck to that, there would be no need for Chitosan. But then, anyone with that sort of superhuman fortitude would be out competing in the Iron Man triathalon, not reading this book.

The way I see it, the ideal eating plan is like a lighthouse, a beacon upon which to set your sights. If you can, I urge you to adhere to the full plan. But do not be too hard on yourself if, in spite of your best efforts, you cannot. For, if you make an honest, continuing effort to eat correctly, if you keep your beacon clearly in view, and you take Chitosan regularly, you will be taking a major step down the road toward keeping your fat intake low, your fiber consumption sufficient, and your cholesterol under control.

As Leo Burnett, the great advertising agent, used to say, "If you reach for the stars, you may not touch one, but you won't come up with a handful of mud either."

With this perspective firmly in view, let us proceed to examine the ideal diet. As you have no doubt gathered, one of its main aspects is that it includes a lot of fruits, vegetables, legumes (beans, peas, lentils, etc.), and very little fat.

Fat Blocker Ideals

Fat:

The daily intake of calories from fat should be no more than 20 percent. This will be easy enough to achieve since Chitosan will help. And it is by far the most important aspect of the entire program.

Protein:

Protein should be kept to about 10 percent of the daily calories.

Carbohydrates:

About 70 percent of the daily calories should come from carbohydrates, almost all of which should be complex (not refined).

Some people believe that this combination of moderate protein, low fat, and high complex carbohydrates is the most difficult part of this or any other diet plan. But in practice, you will find it easier to achieve than you think. That is true for two reasons. The first is that, by the simple expedient of carrying some vegetables with you at all times, you are likely to eat more complex carbohydrates and commensurately less "other stuff," including protein. The second reason is that many meats contain less protein than you might imagine. A lot of their bulk is made up of fat . . . and you've cut down on that with Chitosan. Even the remaining mass is only partially protein. The rest is water (which makes up much of its bulk) and a certain amount of carbohydrates, plus some fiber.

The good news is that if you have slightly more protein than the ideal mix, it probably doesn't matter.

Fiber: Between 35 and 40 grams per day. Again, you help to achieve this automatically with Chitosan.

Water: At least 8 glasses of water per day (do not substitute coffee or tea for water). This is an essential part of the program and you must adhere to it. More about this below.

Cholesterol: Less than 300 mg. should be taken in each day. Again, this is easier to achieve with this program than with any other since Chitosan cuts down on the saturated fat that causes the liver to make more cholesterol.

Salt: No more than 1,000 mg. should be taken in each day. There is a lot of controversy about salt. While everyone agrees that too much is bad, there is a wide discrepancy about what constitutes too much. My view is that 1,000 mg. is ideal, but a bit more is probably not harmful unless you have, or are very prone to, high blood pressure.

If you love salt and wish to cut down, there is an easy way to do this, namely reduce your salt intake very gradually. As you do, you will find that your taste buds get acclimated to less salt. They become more sensitive, and actually taste salt as saltier. If you decrease the amount of salt very slowly, your buds will not notice: Food will taste as salty as before. However, gradually you will become more aware of other flavors. After a few months of this, you will greatly prefer low or even unsalted foods. Excess salt will seem unpleasant. If your doctor tells you to cut down on salt, you can win that fight—as you can the fight for weight loss—without really struggling at all.

A Word About Water

Drinking plenty of water is an integral part of any healthy eating plan. But it is essential when you take Chitosan. In fact, this may be the only rule in this whole book that you should never violate. The reason is that, if you eat a lot of Chitosan and do not drink sufficient water, you may find that you are becoming quite constipated. If this is a situation which becomes extreme (which is very unlikely), you should just cut down on Chitosan. Otherwise, a little constipation is merely annoying. But it should be avoided if possible. And 8 glasses of water a day, in addition to the other benefits it brings, should solve the constipation problem completely.

BUILDING YOUR EATING PROGRAM

How do we develop an eating plan that is practical, doable, and aims in the direction of these ideals? A simple way is to follow the practical, no-nonsense food guide pyramid put out by the U.S. Government. This plan isn't fancy and it doesn't involve hyped-up theories of food combining, or drinking gallons of water, or eating only a couple of kinds of foods. It *is* based on the principles of good old basic nutrition, making it an excellent, easy-to-understand guide to nutritious eating.

When designing your eating program, think about how the ancient Egyptians designed the pyramid. The bulk of the pyramid's bricks were laid at the bottom, with each subsequent layer having fewer and fewer bricks. The same should be true of your

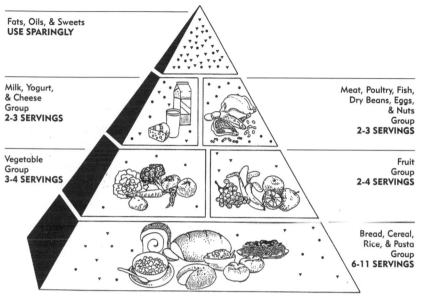

Fats, Oils, & Sweets
USE SPARINGLY

Milk, Yogurt,
& Cheese
Group
2-3 SERVINGS

Meat, Poultry, Fish,
Dry Beans, Eggs,
& Nuts
Group
2-3 SERVINGS

Vegetable
Group
3-4 SERVINGS

Fruit
Group
2-4 SERVINGS

Bread, Cereal,
Rice, & Pasta
Group
6-11 SERVINGS

Food Guide Pyramid

eating plan: Most of your food should come from whole-grain breads, cereals, and pastas, which are the rock-solid basis of a good nutritional program. To this, add lesser amounts (but still plenty) of vegetables and fruits. Working your way up the pyramid, add still smaller amounts of nonfat dairy products and protein foods like meat, fish, poultry, peas, beans, and lentils. Finally, top it off with minimal amounts of fats, oils, and sweets (if desired). Obviously, in practice, this pyramid would often become inverted because we like fats and sweets so much. But you can generally keep to the pattern you seek by the ingestion of Chitosan, shrinking the bulge at the top of the pyramid that would otherwise occur.

How Much Should I Eat?

If you're like most people, it's not enough to hear "Eat lots of this and just a little of that." You want to know exactly how much of each kind of food to eat and why you should eat it in the first place. I'm the same way. You've got to explain it to me—and show me why—before I'll believe anything. So, for those of you who are just like me, here are the details:

The Grain Group *(Bread, Cereal, Rice, and Pasta): 6–11 servings*—The basis of any good eating plan, the grain group provides carbohydrates, energy, fiber, B vitamins, and sometimes iron. Although 6–11 servings sounds like a lot, a typical serving is just one piece of bread, half a cup of cooked rice or pasta, or $1/2$–1 cup of cereal. I always tell my patients to eat whole-grain breads and cereals rather than refined products since they're so much more nutritious and contain a lot more fiber. It's particularly important that you get yourself a good, high-quality bread, since most people get the bulk of their grain servings from bread. Check the label to make sure that the first ingredient is either whole wheat or whole wheat flour. If it says anything else, including enriched flour, find another product. I prefer whole wheat bread with at least 2 grams of fiber per slice. Read the nutritional information on the side of the wrapping. Some brands have as many as 5 grams of fiber per slice. But, of course, if you are eating a lot of Chitosan, you may need less other fiber, and as a fringe benefit of the plan, you may therefore be able to indulge your taste for that crispy French baguette—at least occasionally. After all, there's nothing better than the taste of fresh-baked bread—except maybe the aroma!

Average calorie amount per grain serving: 80

The Vegetable Group: *4–5 servings*—Vegetables add lots of important elements to our diets, including beta carotene (the plant form of vitamin A), vitamin C, folic acid, and other vitamins, plus several minerals and that all-important fiber. Vegetables also contain disease-fighting substances called phytochemicals.

One serving of vegetables is made up of either 1 cup of raw vegetables, a half cup of cooked vegetables or $3/4$ cup of vegetable juice. (Juice should only be counted as 1 serving per day, for it lacks much-needed fiber.) Remember that if you are going to cook your vegetables, you should steam or microwave them lightly (they should still be slightly crisp when served). Raw vegetables make excellent snacks. I always keep my Chitosan bag in full view on my desk to remind me to munch throughout the day.

Unfortunately, some of us get bored with just vegetables. And boredom is a killer. Soon, to overcome our distaste for the same old thing, we find ourselves substituting chocolate truffles or macadamia nuts for carrots and broccoli—and while that dispels the boredom, it does nothing good for our waistlines!

The answer is to make the veggies a little more interesting, at least from time to time, by combining them with a little dip. Excellent low-cal, fat-free dips exist both ready-to-eat in stores and in many good cookbooks. Go ahead, indulge yourself! The extra treat may not be up to the excitement level of a hunk of cheese, but it's very tasty and not hard to live with. (And if you do go for the cheese once in a while, just remember to take some extra Chitosan with it to mitigate its negative effect.)

Average calorie amount per vegetable serving: 25

The Fruit Group: *3–4 servings*—Vitamin C is the biggest contribution made by the fruit group, but fruits also contain good amounts of fiber and other nutrients. Many contain beta carotene, as well as other carotenes. One fruit serving equals 1 medium fruit, a half cup juice, or 1 cup chopped fruit. Once again, only half a cup of juice should be counted toward your fruit allotment per day. If you chop your fruit, make sure you eat it right away because the vitamin content decreases with exposure to air. Fruit is also a great snack and some, like the banana, even come in their own handy, biodegradable wrappers! If your blood sugar tends to rise quickly and then come crashing down, though, it's better not to eat fruit by itself. (The sugar content may wreak havoc on your blood glucose levels.) Eat your fruit along with some nonfat cottage cheese or some high-fiber crackers.

Average calorie amount per fruit serving: 60

The Protein Group *(Meat, Poultry, Fish, Peas, Beans, Lentils, and Eggs): 3 servings*—Back in the 1950s, we thought that we needed plenty of red meat to make us healthy and strong. While I still have nothing against red meat (as long as it's a lean cut, broiled on a rack, and not eaten too often), we now know that most Americans eat way too much protein. An ideal single serving of this group is made up of 3 ounces of cooked, lean meat, poultry, or fish; 1 cup of cooked peas, beans, or lentils; or one egg.

That's not as tough as it seems. Three servings of 3 ounces of meat amounts to a nice chicken breast for lunch and another one for dinner. And you can throw in a cup of peas for your supper, plus (of course) a big baked potato. The reasonable dollop of butter or sour cream necessary to make the potato taste really good will be removed by a couple of grams of Chitosan. All in all, not a bad meal. And, remember, if you eat a little more than you're supposed to, it doesn't matter. As long as you eat a little less than you did before starting the program, and take Chitosan as required, you will lose weight.

Nevertheless, it is desirable to cut down on protein. Do the best you can. Then do a little better . . . because, with my Fat Blocker Program you *can* do it. If you really try, you'll see, your best *is* good enough! To help you cut down on protein to whatever extent you can manage, let me tell you that the average American eats more than twice the protein that he or she needs, which can put the kidneys and liver on overdrive as these organs struggle to excrete

---

Figuring Your Daily Protein Requirement

1. Determine your weight.
2. Multiply your weight by .36.
3. The result equals grams of protein you need each day.

Example:
Weight = 110 lb.
110 × .36 = 39.6 (rounded to 40)
Grams of protein needed per day = 40

---

the excess nitrogen. Too much protein can also bind up much-needed calcium, sending it out of the body through the urine, rather than into the bones where it is vitally needed.

But even though we don't need much protein, it *is* vitally important that we get adequate amounts of it. Protein is necessary for the growth and maintenance of all body tissues, for production of enzymes and hormones, for manufacturing antibodies that fight off foreign invaders, and for maintaining proper fluid, salt, and acid-base balances. Without enough protein, the body will become more and more disease-prone, wasting away as it consumes its own tissues just to stay alive.

For healthy adults, the RDA for protein is .8 grams for each kilogram (2.2 pounds) of body weight. If you're pregnant or recovering from a serious illness, the RDA is higher. And, believe it or not, athletes don't need more protein than the rest of us. Their protein requirements are based on body weight, too, not on activity level. (To figure your own protein requirement, see the box above.)

Besides protein, the protein group provides other essential dietary ingredients such as riboflavin (used in energy-releasing reactions), Vitamin B_6 (used to process amino acids and to release stored glucose), and Vitamin B_{12} (used to produce red blood cells and maintain nerve fiber sheaths).

Keep It Lean!

Trimming the fat, removing the skin, and choosing the leaner cuts of meat and poultry can make the difference between a high fat, high calorie choice and a "slimmer" one. When choosing a cut of red meat, remember that one with the word "round" in its name, such as "round steak," is generally lower in fat.

Average calorie amount per protein serving:

From peas, beans, lentils: 130.

From meat. Lean: 110–165; Medium: 150–225. (There is no point in eating extrafatty meat since lean meat is just as satisfying and tastes just as good. Try a filet mignon instead of a high-fat porterhouse if you don't believe me! And the leaner meat lets you save your Chitosan for when it is really needed.)

The Dairy Group *(Milk, Yogurt, and Cheese): 2–3 servings (I prefer the nonfat varieties)*—This group provides calcium, protein, vitamin D, and other nutrients that are needed for the growth and maintenance of strong bones and connective tissues. A lack of either calcium or vitamin D, which is needed for the proper absorption of calcium, leads to rickets (soft, malformed bones) in children and osteoporosis (hollow bones) in adults.

In recent years, the dairy group has received a lot of undeserved bad press. It's been called everything from mucous producing to unnatural to health threatening. I've found none of these claims to be scientifically substantiated. In fact, the lack of dairy products (and resulting lack of calcium) seems to be a lot more threatening to the health. Adequate amounts of calcium are vital for children and adolescents who are actively building bones and for pregnant women who are supporting the growth of the fetal skeleton. Without it, the quality of the bone suffers, paving the way for osteoporosis later in life. In my 40 years of medical practice, I've seen many patients suffering from this disease. Their brittle, easily broken bones are constantly wracked with pain, making it extremely difficult to get around. Eventually, the victim is confined to bed. The confinement, in turn, brings on complications such as pneumonia and other diseases that prey on the inactive. Not only do osteoporosis sufferers tend to die more quickly than their peers, the quality of their lives is severely lessened by the disease. So remember what your mother used to tell you: "Drink your milk!"

One serving of the dairy group is equal to 1 cup of milk, $1^1/_2$ ounces of natural cheese, or 1 cup of yogurt. Of course, dairy products all suffer one disadvantage for dieters, they contain a lot of fat. For example, most cheese gets as much as 80 percent of its calories from fat, and cream cheese gets 91 percent. You can always try nonfat cheese, and for certain purposes (such as very spicy pizza where the taste and consistency of the cheese is largely masked), nonfat cheese can be quite acceptable. But to eat a chunk of the stuff plain may seem to you like eating soft plastic or candle wax. So, instead, eat a small amount of the cheese you really like, a little less than you usually eat, and pull out the excess fat with an extra gram or 2 of Chitosan.

The same approach applies to skim milk, which is my favorite, the only kind I drink. If you really dislike it, and even the low-fat 1 percent milk is too watery for your taste, try 2 percent—and a little Chitosan.

I do recommend nonfat yogurt. It tastes almost as delicious as ice cream, and it lets you save Chitosan for when you really need it.

Average calorie amount per dairy serving. Nonfat: 90; Low-fat: 120.

The Extra Group *(Fats, Oils, and Sweets): Use sparingly—* Saturated fat (the kind found in animal products, pies, pastries, and other goodies) is just about the worst thing for your diet. As I have explained, it is especially bad for the heart and has been implicated in the cancer process. Luckily, it is also electro-negatively charged and therefore sticks to Chitosan just as iron filings do to a magnet. This is where Chitosan is such a godsend. So, use low- or no-fat substitutes where they taste good. For example, there are lots of good-tasting nonfat and low-fat salad dressings, baked goods, and mayonnaises available. But when you want an occasional piece of chocolate, some popcorn *with* butter at the movies, or a hot dog at the ball park (and who can resist those things all the time?), eat them in small amounts and take Chitosan about 30 minutes in advance to help offset all the dangers of excess fat.

The Fluid Group *(Primarily water): at least 8 servings a day—*Adults need a minimum of 8, 8-ounce glasses of plain water every day to keep their bodies properly hydrated. Plain water means just water, not coffee, tea, soda, etc.

Generally speaking, 60 percent of a man's body weight is made up of water, compared to about 50 percent in women. This wonderful, versatile substance is used in virtually every bodily function. But most of us live in a state of chronic low-level dehydration, resulting in impaired transport of vital nutrients and enzymes through the body. To conserve water, the body begins to produce histamine, which some medical practitioners believe is the source of many cases of bronchitis, headaches, joint pains, depression, indigestion, high blood pressure, backaches, and fatigue. Lack of water can also result in increased water retention, which shows up on the body in the form of unattractive bloating and extra pounds.

When you take Chitosan, the problem of insufficient water may be compounded, as I have already noted, by your becoming constipated, especially when you are just starting on your Fat Blocker Program.

Fortunately, the remedy for lack of water is really simple—just drink at least 2 quarts of water each day. Many of my patients who are always tired are amazed at how well they feel when they drink these 8 glasses of water daily. Don't wait until you're thirsty to drink your water. Most experts believe that the body needs water long before thirst appears. And don't try to drink it all at once! Regular sipping throughout the day ensures easier absorption and maximum hydrating effects. I find that keeping a big bottle of water on my desk reminds me to keep refilling my glass and drinking throughout the day. I also find it helps keep my appetite under control. And this inexpensive, effective weight loss/health aid is as close as your nearest tap. Drink up!

By the way, our ability to recognize thirst decreases with age. That's why some older people suffer from a marked decline in mental acuity and physical abilities—they're not drinking enough water. I've treated many people with these problems who responded simply to drinking more water and drinking it regularly throughout the day, not waiting until they finally feel thirsty.

Remember: Don't wait until you're thirsty to begin drinking water. By the time you feel really thirsty, you've most likely already lost 1–2 percent of your body fluids. If you feel tired and weak, if your physical performance has deteriorated, you've probably lost about 3 percent of your body fluids. Don't wait. Drink at least 8, 8-ounce glasses of water (2 quarts) a day.

How Many Servings Should I Have?

I've told you what kinds of foods to eat, but I've given it to you in a range. For example, it's recommended that you eat 6–11 servings of the grain group each day. "Well," you may say, "there's a big difference between eating 6 pieces of bread and 11! Which is it?" To figure out just how much is right for you, ask yourself a couple of questions: How big are you? (Are you a 6' 4" 250-pound man or a 4' 10" 85-pound teenage girl?) How active are you? (Do you spend your days training for the Olympic gymnastic trials, or do you sit at a computer most of the day?) How different is the Fat Blocker Eating Program from the way you're used to eating? (Is this going to be a big change, or do you normally eat like this?) How quickly do you want to lose weight? (Would you rather get it off in a hurry or take the slow-but-sure course?) Finally, how big is your appetite? (Do you regularly gobble up anything that isn't moving, or is your appetite more restrained?)

In general, smaller,

Variety Is Vital!

You should never use just one type of food for *all* of your servings from a food group (for example, 6 pieces of bread). The greater the variety of foods, the better your chances of getting all the vitamins, minerals, and other good things that your body needs. And the choices are practically limitless! In the grain group alone you can choose from wheat, rye, rice, barley, oats, wild rice, corn, or millet, among others. And these grains can take the form of bread, crackers, tortillas, pita bread, chapatis, and a host of different kinds of pasta. Experiment a little—it makes life more interesting!

less active people with normal appetites should eat the lower number of recommended servings, while larger, more active people who are used to eating a lot should go for the larger number of servings. If you're particularly hungry one day, eat the larger number of servings; if your appetite is low, eat the smaller number.

The faster you want to lose weight, the fewer servings you should eat, *but do not eat fewer than the lowest number of recommended servings.* Eating less means cheating your body of much-needed nutrients and can actually slow your metabolism. That's because your body thinks it has entered a starvation state. Panicked, it shifts into low gear to conserve its energy and begins to burn calories much more slowly. Then, once you start to eat more (which is bound to happen), you'll find that your body has gotten very good at making body fat. It's still conserving every single calorie that it can, even though the starvation state may be long past. So keep eating—you'll be thinner (and healthier) in the long run.

Keep Your Heart Healthy!

If you eat the kinds and quantities of foods outlined in my modified food guide pyramid, including the Chitosan, of course, you'll probably be able to stay within the Fat Blocker guidelines for protein, carbohydrate, and certainly for fat. That leaves just two other things to watch out for: cholesterol and sodium.

Everybody knows that high blood cholesterol is a risk factor for heart disease. Cholesterol is a major component of plaque, a substance that contains fat and accumulates on the walls of arteries, clogging these vessels the way hair clogs up bathroom pipes. And remember when you pull the fat out of plaque, the body can do a better job of dilating the blood vessels.

About 75 percent of our blood cholesterol is manufactured by the liver, with the other 25 percent coming from the foods we eat. The major dietary cause of high blood cholesterol is saturated fat. If you're following the Fat Blocker Eating Program,

you're eating only rea-
sonable amounts of lean
meats, poultry, and fish,
and many of your dairy
products are low- or non-
fat. More important, you
are also blocking a large
percentage of your satu-
rated fat with Chitosan.
As a result, saturated fat
intake shouldn't be a
problem for you. But for
some people, blood cho-
lesterol increases when

What Is Saturated Fat?

Saturated fats come from meat and animal products. We also make saturated fats by turning oil, such as corn oil, into solids such as margarine. All saturated fats cause the body to make more cholesterol. Cakes, pies, and pastries are usually filled with saturated fat.

they eat cholesterol-containing foods, even ones that contain relatively little saturated fat. Among the biggest offenders are egg
yolks, organ meats (liver, kidney, heart, brains, sweetbreads),
and certain shellfish (shrimp and oysters).

One egg contains as much cholesterol (300 mg.) as you actually need in a day. So try to limit yourself to no more than one
egg per day, and no more than three eggs per week. This can be
difficult since this includes eggs in baked goods or other foods.
However, if you exceed your limit, don't worry too much. Now
that you're on a Chitosan diet, at least you know that you're not
building more cholesterol from absorbing excess saturated fat.

Also, it's useful to take some other precautions against taking
in excess cholesterol. For example, I eat only the whites of the
eggs to ensure that I consume no cholesterol. I love a simple
omelet made with egg whites, vegetables, and spices. It tastes
excellent and requires virtually no fat to cook, thus letting me
save Chitosan for other things that do require fat. Also, when I
eat a high-cholesterol meal, I try to make the rest of the meals
that day vegetarian. Even if you don't quite succeed in this, the
attempt is worth the effort. For remember, you are not expecting
to instantly achieve the ideal diet, only one that is a step closer
to the ideal than you were yesterday!

High-sodium diets can contribute to another heart disease

risk factor—hypertension, better known as high blood pressure. Called the silent killer because it produces no symptoms in the early stages, high blood pressure can exert enough pressure on your arteries to cause tiny cracks to appear in their walls. Clots and plaque can form in the cracks, and before you know it, you've got the makings of a heart attack or stroke. Sodium in excessive quantity can cause blood pressure to rise in certain sensitive individuals, eventually leading to heart enlargement and congestive heart failure. We doctors have many medicines to lower blood pressure, but they all have side effects. Perhaps the best medicine is to avoid the problem altogether by reducing your salt intake. As I described earlier, if you do this *very* gradually, it is not hard to do.

Some diets recommend lowering your salt level by going cold turkey and just throwing your salt shaker away so you won't be tempted to add salt to your food at the table. If that works for you, great. But if it doesn't, the slow-and-easy method described earlier works, too. And it's in line with my thinking about Chitosan. It's better to go real slow and easy, making tiny changes regularly and helping yourself along with Chitosan, than it is to take huge steps only, inevitably, to stumble and fall.

Whether you use the gradual or the cold turkey approach to cutting down on salt, sooner or later you will want to keep the salt you use in cooking to a minimum. Put in half the amount the recipe calls for, or even less. Stay away from salty foods such as smoked, pickled, or cured foods, canned soups, frozen dinners, salad dressings, catsup, baked goods, crackers, chips, or salted popcorn. Eat fresh vegetables and fruits, not canned. After a while, you'll find that your old favorites suddenly taste much too salty. And you'll discover the more delicate, true tastes of food.

The Splurge Allotment

We're all human, and that means that none of us can be perfect *all* the time. When it comes to eating, despite our best intentions, we sometimes get the urge to splurge. Fortunately, splurging can be a good thing, at least up to a point. Psychologists have found that allowing for some imperfection, whether it's in dieting, exercising, or accomplishing any difficult task, helps us stick to the task in the long run. In context with the Fat Blocker Eating Program, occasional treats are easy to deal with because you can use Chitosan to block the fat and hence some of the calories and unhealthy side effects of the fat in these treats. The long-term result is that you can stay on the rest of your sensible eating plan much more easily—and the splurge ends up doing you more good than harm.

I should warn, however, that there are two potential pitfalls to splurging. One is that you have to be careful to avoid a splurge becoming an all-out binge. One piece of cheesecake is fine; an entire cheesecake is not desirable! That's why we should approach these foods with caution. I like to figure out in advance what my treat will be, when I'm going to eat it, and how much of it I'll eat. Then I take the appropriate amount of Chitosan before eating the splurge food. If I'm ordering my treat in a restaurant, I also decide in advance how much of it I'm going to eat. I remove the excess *before* I start to eat and have the waiter take it away.

The other risk with splurging is that we get to rely so much on Chitosan's ability to negate the negative of fat that we keep splurging. Inevitably, that means we'll gain weight. For the Chitosan never absorbs *all* the fat we consume. For one thing, you can't eat enough Chitosan to eliminate all the fat you can consume if you are really overeating. The practical maximum of Chitosan you can take before a meal is about 4 grams. At most, that will eliminate 24 grams of fat. But a McDonald's Big Mac contains about double that. So, if you eat as many cheeseburgers as before and eat your Chitosan, you'll cut down on fat, calories, and weight. But if you splurge regularly on extra Big Macs, you'll gain weight, and probably lots of it.

Setting It Up—The Meal Plan

In my many years of experience with weight-loss patients, I've found that 3 meals and 2 snacks per day work a lot better than 3 meals alone. The body seems to speed up its metabolism when it realizes it's getting fed on a regular basis, with brief periods of fasting time in between. And it's easier both physically and psychologically to stay with the plan. The number one enemy of the overweight health seeker—hunger—is banished!

To show you how easily the Fat Blocker guidelines can be translated into menus, I've set up 2 of them: one for the smaller amount of servings and one for the larger. One or the other, or something in between, should be just right for you.

Plan I

The Minimum Amount of Servings

Breakfast

　　1 serving grain group
　　1 serving dairy group
　　1 serving fruit group

Lunch

　　2 servings grain group
　　1 serving protein group
　　1 serving vegetable group

Snack

　　1 serving grain group
　　1 serving vegetable group

Dinner

　　2 servings grain group
　　1 serving protein group
　　1 serving vegetable group

Snack

　　1 serving fruit group
　　1 serving dairy group

　　Total Calorie Count (without added fats, oils, or sweets) = 1400

PLAN II

The Maximum Amount of Servings

BREAKFAST

>   2 servings grain group
>   1 serving dairy group
>   1 serving fruit group

LUNCH

>   2 servings grain group
>   1 serving protein group
>   2 servings vegetable group
>   1 serving fruit group
>   1 serving dairy group

SNACK

>   2 servings grain group
>   1 serving fruit group

DINNER

>   3 servings grain group
>   2 servings protein group
>   3 servings vegetable group
>   1 serving dairy group

SNACK

>   1 serving fruit group
>   2 servings grain group

>   Total Calorie Count (without added fats, oils, or sweets) =
>   2100

Of course, these menu plans assume that you take in no Chito-san. If you take, say, 3 grams of Chitosan during the day for Plan I and 6 grams for Plan II that will eliminate between 9 and 18 grams of fat (or 80 to 160 calories) for Plan I and between 18 and 36 grams of fat (or 160 to 325 calories) for Plan II. Since without that reduction these plans are sufficient for most people to lose weight, with the Chitosan you can afford an extra splurge now and then—even if you are on an ideal diet.

If you are not on the ideal plan, but working your way towards that beacon, all you have to do is eat the same as before, but cut down slightly by using your Chitosan bag, keep the splurging to the level you've always enjoyed, and let the Chitosan be your basic calorie reduction mechanism. Although you eat just a little bit less each day, your body will absorb quite a bit less, and so you'll lose weight.

The Splurge

Splurges should be carefully planned and reasonably infrequent. If you let Chitosan enable you to splurge more often than you used to, you will undo all of your good efforts. Splurges are difficult to categorize because by their nature they are spontaneous. In general, however, I feel that you should try to limit them to no more than 20 grams of fat and a maximum of 300 extra calories. (If the splurge contains food groups from the Eating Program, the extra calories you should count are those above and beyond what you typically eat. For example, at lunch your plan may call for 1 serving of meat and 2 grains, which would equal 270 calories. If you decide to have a hamburger instead, which contains 330 calories, your extras would only amount to about 60 calories). Of course, since most of that extra is fat, 1 or 2 grams of Chitosan will take care of it.

To help you with your planning, use this list of typical treats that might be used for a splurge, including the fat and calorie amounts that they contain.

Food	Grams of Fat in Food	Calories Contained	Add Chitosan	Grams of Fat Avoided	Calories Avoided
Fritos corn chips, 1 oz.	10	160	2 g.	10	90
apple pie, 1 slice	15	310	3 g.	15	135
chocolate sundae	7	300	1 g.	5	255
cheese pizza, thin crust, 1/3 of 12" pie	16	360	3 g.	15	135
french fries, 1 small order	10	210	2 g.	10	90
(McDonald's) Quarter Pounder hamburger	20	420	4 g.	20	180
chocolate shake, small	6	350	1 g.	5	45
(Wendy's) broccoli & cheese baked potato	14	460	2 g.	10	90
butter, 1 tbsp.	11	100	2 g.	10	90
Häagen-Dazs, ice cream, 1/2 cup	18	270	3 g.	15	135
(Stouffer's) lasagna with meat sauce	13	360	2 g.	10	90
cashew halves, 1 oz.	14	170	2 g.	10	90
pork sausage, 2 oz.	20	250	4 g.	20	180
(Marie's) blue cheese dressing, 2 tbsp.	19	180	3 g.	15	135
(Lay's) potato chips, 20 chips (28 g.)	10	150	2 g.	10	90

These figures assume each gram of Chitosan blocks 5 grams of fat (equal to 45 calories).

In Summary

So there you have the Fat Blocker Eating Program, which I truly believe is the very best way to eat. A billionaire who could afford to hire his own team of scientists and nutritionists couldn't end up with a better, more nutritious diet than this. Yet it's simple, easy to follow, and all of the foods are readily available at your local grocery store. All that's necessary is a little advance planning. Keep healthful foods at hand, prepare dishes in advance for quick reheating, and bring food along with you when you're not sure what will be available. It's when we're unprepared that we tend to grab whatever food is nearby—and that's when we have problems.

But, above all, don't forget to bring the Chitosan. Without that, you will be in trouble. And only the traditional draconian diet (the ideal that shows us the way but may never actually be achieved) will be enough to save you. Without Chitosan, you'll be back trying to attain an impossible dream. With Chitosan, you'll be able to lose weight in the real world.

7

◆

Supplements and Eating Tips

What About Supplements?

Even though the Fat Blocker Eating Program is the most nutritious way you can possibly eat, I still recommend that you take supplements of the antioxidant vitamins and minerals. Volumes of research have shown that antioxidants can help ward off cancer, heart disease, and many other diseases, and can even slow the aging process. But we simply don't get enough of these vitamins and minerals in our diets. So supplements seem to be the way to go. Remember, though, that supplements should never be substituted for nutritious eating. They add to your diet, they don't replace it!

Note: While on my 8-Point Fat Blocker Program, it's best to take your supplements with breakfast and an hour or two *after* your evening meal. Doing so eliminates any risk of the Chitosan you may be taking with lunch or dinner pulling certain fat-soluble nutrients out of your stomach before they can be absorbed.

What Are Antioxidants?

In recent years, scientists discovered that certain unstable molecules called free radicals roam through the body attacking and destroying healthy tissue. A free radical molecule becomes unstable because it has lost an electron. Think of it as sort of a loose cannon that careens around, interacting with other molecules in a destructive way. It really wants to stabilize itself, and to do that it will often steal an electron from another molecule. But this undermines the second molecule, making *it* into a free radical that spins off in search of an electron to grab from another molecule. It's sort of like a destructive game of tag (I steal from you, you steal from the next guy). You can imagine how cells, tissues, and organs become permanently damaged by this rampant stealing.

Luckily, we can fight the effects of free radicals with the antioxidants. The antioxidants get their name by fighting one of the most common free radicals found in the body—oxygen. That's right, the same thing we must breathe to survive can also be the thing that does some of the greatest damage to our bodies. Except that this is a special form of oxygen called singlet oxygen. Oxygen molecules, including those we breathe, usually travel in groups of two (O_2). But sometimes, during the normal metabolic processes in the body, the twosome splits. The two new molecules are singlet oxygen. Each is missing an electron, so each becomes a roving free radical. Fortunately, the antioxidants are able to stabilize singlet oxygen and prevent it from wreaking havoc on bodily tissues.

The antioxidants include beta carotene and other carotenes (the plant form of the vitamin A), vitamin C, vitamin E, and the mineral selenium. An easy way to remember them is to think of them as the 4 ACES we discussed before. As with all nutrients, it's better to get them in their natural state, as a part of your foods, because they're absorbed better and they work together with other substances contained in the food. Still, numerous studies have shown that supplements (when used in addition to a good diet) can help protect the body. So, I regularly recommend them to my patients. Below I've listed some sources of each of the 4 ACES, as well as the amount of supplementation that, after years of experience, I believe to be the best.

✦ **Vitamin A: beta carotene and other carotenes**—Good sources of vitamin A include yellow-orange fruits and vegetables such as sweet potatoes, apricots, pumpkins, carrots, cantaloupes, and other melons, mangoes, papaya, peaches, and winter squash. Dark green leafy vegetables such as broccoli, spinach, collard greens, parsley, and other leafy greens are also good sources.

Supplement:

I typically recommend to my patients 25,000 IU daily of beta carotene. Better still, at most health food stores you can purchase combination supplements that contain beta carotene plus alpha carotene, lutein, lycopene, zeaxanthin, and cryptoxanthin. Use the amounts as directed on the label. However, rest assured even if you make a mistake and eat more than the recommended amounts, it makes little difference. Our bodies need food supplements in certain amounts. A reasonable excess simply has no place and gets eliminated. This does not mean, however, that you should eat far more than recommended. Serious overdoses of such nutrients as vitamin A can be dangerous.

✦ **Vitamin C**—Probably the best known of all of the vitamins, this antioxidant is found in citrus fruits, cantaloupes, papayas, kiwis, mangoes, raspberries, pineapples, bananas, and strawberries. It's also found in lots of fresh vegetables such as asparagus, brussels sprouts, collard greens, cabbage, broccoli, tomatoes, potatoes, and red peppers. Vitamin C is heat sensitive and easily destroyed by cooking or exposure to air, so fruits and vegetables should be as fresh as possible, and if cooked, should be steamed or microwaved only a short time. You can keep the vitamin C in cooked foods longer by cooking them whole and cutting them up afterwards, rather than before.

Supplement:

I generally recommend starting with 500–1000 mg. of vitamin C twice a day.

✦ **Vitamin E**—Vegetable oils (such as sunflower and saf-flower) are the main source of vitamin E, but it's also found in wheat germ, nuts, avocados, peaches, sunflower seeds, whole grain breads and cereals, spinach, broccoli, asparagus, dried prunes, and peanut butter.

Supplement:

I don't believe that you can get enough vitamin E from the diet alone. In any case, eating that amount of peanut butter is hardly a good idea! That's why I often recommend to my patients that they start with between 300–400 IU twice a day. I take my vitamin E in the form of 400 IU of D-alpha tocopherol succinate, twice a day.

✦ **Selenium**—This antioxidant not only helps protect the cells from the damaging effects of free radicals, but may also help keep the immune system functioning properly. Good amounts of selenium can be found in swordfish, salmon, tuna, cracked wheat bread, sunflower seeds, oysters, and shrimp.

Supplement:

I usually suggest to my patients that they take 200 mcg. per day. Recent studies published in the *Journal of the American Medical Association*[1] show that selenium can prevent almost all cancerous tumors (except skin cancer).

Vitamins A, C, and E, plus selenium, are not the only antioxidants. These substances are powerful partners for the 4 ACES:

✦ **Alpha lipotene** (a brand of alpha lipoic acid)—The most powerful universal metabolic antioxidant.

✦ **Coenzyme Q10**—Helps each cell make energy, also a strong antioxidant.

✦ **Proanthocyanidins**—Flavonoids which have a powerful antioxidant and anti–heart attack effect. Pycnogenol is a standardized form of the proanthocyanidins which comes from the bark of the Pinus pinaster in France.

✦ **Epigallocatechin gallate**—A very strong antioxidant with anticancer and anti–cardiovascular disease properties, found in Japanese green tea.

Other nutrients I have found to be of value for the Fat Blocker Eating Program include zinc, the B-complex vitamins, and magnesium. I generally recommend that my patients take

✦ **Alpha lipotene**—50 mg. twice a day.

✦ **Coenzyme Q10**—30 mg. once daily, taken with the largest meal, if you're under 50. If you're over 50 and have absolutely no health problems, 100 mg. once a day. If you're over 50 and have high blood pressure and/or heart disease, 200 mg. once a day.

✦ **Proanthocyanidins/Pycnogenol**—30 mg. twice a day.

✦ **Epigallocatechin gallate**—I suggest drinking 2–3 glasses of Japanese green tea a day to get epigallocatechin gallate.

✦ **Zinc**—20 mg. once daily.

✦ **B-complex vitamins**—A B-complex containing 50 mg. of the major B vitamins (B_1, B_2, B_3, B_5, B_6), plus B_{12}, and folic acid twice daily.

✦ **Magnesium**—300–350 mg. twice a day.

Now, the problem with taking all these supplements is obvious. It's too complicated. And, as you will have seen so far, I believe in simplicity. Fortunately, there is a simple answer in this case. It lies in the fact that several brands of multivitamins exist that contain many or all of these recommended products. If you cannot find any of these brands in your local store, I suggest you ask your physician or nutritionist to suggest other appropriate products. Also, I should add that, as with my other recommendations, these are only general guidelines for supplements. Talk to your physician or nutritionist for your specific needs.

Helpful Hints for Taking Off the Pounds—And Keeping Them Off!

In weight loss and weight management, like so many other things in life, it's the little things that count. I tell my overweight patients *not* to make sudden, huge changes in their habits. Instead, start with little ones. You don't have to stop eating all of your favorite foods at once. Begin by eating one less cookie than you normally would. Order a sandwich without mayonnaise, for a change. Have an extra serving of vegetables. If you start to change your habits slowly, you'll probably find that it's not so painful at all. Like a snowball rolling down a hill, one good habit can build and become a whole host of good habits. So don't be hard on yourself. Life is for living! Just do better than before. That, and Chitosan, will get you where you want to be.

To help you on your way, consider the following tips for successful eating:

1. **Try not to skip meals**—As I've mentioned before, skipping meals can set you up for overeating later on. It can also lower your metabolic rate, which translates to a faster weight gain and a harder time getting it off. So keep eating regularly—at least three meals, coupled with the requisite Chitosan for the larger ones, plus two snacks per day.

2. **Don't constantly count calories**—Although I've given calorie counts for the 2 examples of meal plans that were given earlier in this chapter, that was just for general reference. I discourage my patients from counting calories throughout the day because it puts an emphasis on the energy content of a food, instead of its nutritional content. (According to a calorie counter, a roast beef sandwich is the same as a hot fudge sundae! Nutrition-

ally, of course, there's a big difference.) In any case, given that the Chitosan you are eating will be eliminating an unspecified number of fat calories, counting total calorie intake is a waste of time: You won't know how many more calories you are getting from sugar, compared to how many you are saving from fat. Instead, count servings from the food groups since that assures you of a correct intake balance. Then use the Chitosan to avoid the excess fat.

3. **Always eat sitting down**—Andy Warhol once said that his favorite meal was a peanut butter sandwich eaten while standing over the sink. Well, we've all done it, we've all gobbled up a lot of high-fat, high-sugar foods while standing there. (It's almost as if we think it won't count if we eat it fast enough!) Don't fool yourself. The more relaxed you are, the more slowly you'll eat, the more you'll enjoy your food, the better your digestive system will perform, and most likely, the more nutritious your meal will be. In addition, I suspect that eating slowly will give the Chitosan in your stomach a better opportunity to attract the fat and carry it away.

4. **Eat a variety of foods**—Boredom is one of the primary reasons that many people abandon an eating program. They get tired of eating the same old things over and over again. Consequently, they switch to something else—which is usually a combination of pizza, doughnuts, and maybe a couple of beers! (I remember one diet that consisted of bacon, eggs, and grapefruit 3 times a day for as long as you could stand it. People did lose weight on this diet, probably because they just didn't want to eat very much after the first few days. But, of course, they soon started eating something else and regained the lost weight in no time.) So, experiment: Try new dishes, new foods, new combinations. The more interesting you make your food, the more likely you are to feel satisfied by it and not switch to something that isn't good for you. (Yes, it's okay to splurge occasionally, but when you do, enjoy it—try not to waste your splurge

on leftovers because you got bored with your main meal.)

5. **Tune into your body's signals**—Many of my patients who have been chronic dieters are completely out of touch with their body's signals. This probably occurs because they learn to ignore hunger when dieting rigorously, and soon they learn to ignore satiety (the feeling of fullness) too. They get so tied up in the psychological side of eating ("I *have* to have this!" and "I *can't* have this!") that their bodily responses become secondary.

   Start listening to your body's signals again. Try to determine whether or not you're really hungry. When you feel the urge to eat, if it's not mealtime, wait 10 minutes. Perhaps the pang you felt wasn't really a signal that you need to eat. If, after 10 minutes you're still hungry, snack from your Chitosan bag. If your hunger persists after that, eat. When you do eat, enjoy something that's part of the plan. Eat the food, then wait 20 minutes. Chances are the hunger will be gone. When eating a meal, chew slowly and try to concentrate on the sensations in your mouth, throat, and stomach. The minute you feel a hint of fullness, stop! You can always come back to the meal later, but right now you're trying to train yourself to pick up cues. Leave the table for 20 minutes; go get involved in another activity. Then, if you're still hungry, come back and eat some more. The goal is to be able to rely on your body to tell you when and how much to eat. We were all born with this ability, but many of us have lost it somewhere along the way.

6. **Slow down**—Did you know that it takes at least 20 minutes from the time you start eating for the feeling of satiety to set in? The faster you eat, the more food you can pack away before your body tells you it's had enough. Adopt a leisurely pace as you eat your food. You'll enjoy it more and slim down at the same time.

7. **Eat with a friend**—While we're on the subject of eating slowly, have you ever noticed how much longer it takes you to finish a meal when you're engrossed in conversa-

tion with a good friend? The company of friends or family members can make a meal much more pleasurable, and can keep you from eating too fast or obsessing about your food. You'll feel more satisfied at the end of the meal because you've been filled not only with food, but also with good cheer.

8. **Get organized**—Bring food with you when you're not sure what will be available. I know a woman who used to bring her own special cucumber soup in a thermos to a restaurant. She also had little individual packets of low-fat salad dressing, some whole wheat crackers and a plastic bag of cut-up vegetables with her at all times. Frankly, I think for most of us, that may be going a little far. There is no point in being obsessive about losing weight. It won't last. But taking your Chitosan bag with you does make sense. And, occasionally, say when you visit your heavy-eating brother, it may make sense to bring some of your own food with you. In any case, do bring the Chitosan. (Maybe your brother would like some too!) When you do eat out, watch the portion sizes (they're usually huge), trim your meat, poultry, or fish of any visible fat, and limit extras such as sauces and dressings. Ask for single items rather than combination dishes, and for a side of whole-grain bread rather than the fatty breads and rolls usually offered.

9. **Limit your alcohol intake**—I used to tell my patients to watch their alcohol intake. Then a patient told me, laughing, "Yeah, I watch my alcohol intake. I watch it being poured into my glass, I watch it as I lift the glass to my mouth and drink it." Now I say limit your alcohol intake. In modest quantities alcohol is good for you. There is a huge amount of research, some of it conducted by various governments (including the United States), showing that up to $1^1/_2$ ounces of pure alcohol per day (that is about two drinks) significantly lowers your bad cholesterol levels, and spread out over a few hours, not taken on an empty stomach, and not prior to driving, lengthens your life expectancy by several years.

On the other hand, alcohol contains plenty of calories, so use it sensibly.

10. **Be realistic**—Most of us, including me, are not going to follow any plan perfectly. The more strict you are with yourself, the more likely you'll be to abandon the plan altogether. As I've said before, just making the effort can do wonders for your body and your overall health.

Get Started Now!

There's no time like the present to get started. The essential first step, of course, is to stock up on Chitosan. It is available in almost any good health food store, and through a number of mail order companies.

The second step is to stock your kitchen with healthful foods. Here's a list of some foods to keep in your kitchen and use often:

- ✦ **Fruits**—apples, oranges, grapefruit, kiwis, bananas, pears, peaches, nectarines.

- ✦ **Cereals**—Shredded Wheat, Grape Nuts, rolled oats, oat bran, bran flakes.

- ✦ **Dairy Products**—skim (nonfat) milk, eggs (use only the whites), nonfat yogurt, farmer's cheese, pot cheese, hoop cheese, nonfat buttermilk, nonfat cottage cheese, freshly grated parmesan cheese.

- ✦ **Grains**—barley, brown rice, wild rice, popcorn (nonfat, unsalted), rye flour, buckwheat (kasha), polenta, couscous.

- ✦ **Peas, Beans, and Lentils**—lima beans, pinto beans, black beans, peas, lentils, garbanzo beans, great northern white beans, navy beans.

- ✦ **Vegetables**—broccoli, brussels sprouts, cabbage, cauliflower, spinach, green peppers, red peppers, mushrooms, onions, tomatoes, romaine lettuce, soybeans (in the pod), radishes, eggplant, carrots, celery, parsley, zucchini, potatoes, sweet potatoes, turnips, asparagus, cucumbers, fresh ginger, beets. If you must use canned vegetables, purchase unsalted varieties.

✦ **Pasta**—whole wheat lasagna noodles, spinach pasta, whole wheat spaghetti, whole wheat macaroni, egg-free noodles.

✦ **Bread**—whole wheat bread, rolls, and pita bread.

Happy—and healthful—eating!

8

---◆---

The Fat Blocker Exercise Program

Debbie is a 42-year-old married mother of 2 who works part-time as a secretary while going to college. Always a bit chubby, even as a girl, she recently found herself about 30 pounds over-weight. "I'm really pretty good about my eating," she told me. "I watch the fat, I eat small portions and hardly ever have dessert. I'm *sure* I eat less than any of my friends. So why can't I lose the weight?" When I asked her about her exercising habits, she said, "When do I have time to exercise? I'm either working, at school, taking care of the kids, or studying. I just can't seem to fit it into my schedule!"

A basic truth that I've discovered after years of treating over-weight patients is this: We cannot achieve permanent weight loss without exercise. Every living being exercises to some extent. Even breathing is a form of exercise. And our heart is a muscle that never ceases to work out. However, our bodies are designed to do a great deal more exercise than that. Just as we evolved to consume any food we could lay our hands on, so we also evolved in circumstances where we often had to expend a great burst of energy. Even when energy (i.e., food) is in short supply, it's worth using up a large store of it to evade a saber-toothed tiger, or to hunt down a buffalo. Those bursts of energy were once essential for our survival. However, once the danger was past or the prey captured, there was no further advantage in using up energy. So, we learned to relax and shut down, our stomachs full, our fat building up for future emergencies. In those prehistoric days, we maintained a sensible balance between energy usage and energy storage.

Today, since there are no tigers to flee from and we can obtain all the food we could possibly want with no more energy than it takes to push a cart through a supermarket, our tendency to store energy (i.e., fat) is far greater than our need to expend it. We are out of balance, and that problem has to be dealt with.

The obvious solution is to exercise in bursts of high energy several times a week. Most experts believe that exercising for at least 30 minutes at least 4 times a week is needed to keep the body in good shape, and 5 times a week for at least 45 minutes is considered optimal. That is not so tough to do under normal conditions, and many people who are serious about keeping their good health and want to keep their weight down do manage it. (Remember, that includes the pickup basketball game, moving furniture to rearrange the living room, and shoveling snow.) In addition, low-energy exercise, when added to the impact of high-energy bursts, also helps to consume calories. Walking a few blocks instead of driving can help balance intake and output.

Some people may find it difficult to stick to even a relatively doable exercise program while dieting. They find that the body wants to take it easy. "Hey, isn't there a good movie on TV?" it asks as they begin to put on their track shoes. "Oh, and while you're up, why not make some popcorn? And not that air-popped stuff either!"

We may resist for a while, but for many of us, the temptation becomes too great and we succumb to behavior that while admittedly unhealthy in today's world, was entirely appropriate over the course of our 2 million years of struggling for survival.

Fortunately, reducing caloric intake with Chitosan circumvents this standard bodily slow-down reaction. Our bodies remain comfortable with the same amount of exercise they did before. Even a reasonable amount of added exercise is no great burden. As a result, the whole regimen of calorie reduction becomes effective.

Now a new and thoroughly pleasing effect starts to be felt: As our bodies lose fat and become lighter, they function better. We feel healthier. If our joints have a touch of osteoarthritis, they feel less stiff because they carry less weight. Since we are carting fewer pounds of fat around, we have more energy to spare for other things. The result of all this is that it becomes easier to exercise more. Perhaps we jog an extra lap, or finally get around to building that tool shed, or even have enough spare energy to work out an extra day a week. Or maybe we get up earlier in the morning and spend an hour a day just moving around more. Whatever we do, that extra energy expenditure naturally uses up calories and further reduces our weight.

The effect of Chitosan, then, is to help replace the vicious circle of weight gain with a positive circle of weight reduction: Less caloric accretion causes us to lose weight, lower weight gives us spare energy, more energy causes us to do more exercise to burn off more calories, and that results in our losing more weight. Excellent! The only question is, where does it stop?

Most people do well when 10–25 percent of the body weight comes from fat. (Ten to 15 percent is a good range for men, with women doing well in the 20 to 25 percent range.) More than that and we are accumulating unnecessary fat. Once we drop down to minimum levels, the body will not easily give up additional fat. Short of virtual starvation (including anorexia and Ghandi-like asceticism, both of which are akin to starvation from the body's point of view) it will not drop below that minimum. Even with continued Chitosan consumption before meals—probably necessary to maintain that svelte new you—nothing more happens.

Let me repeat, one thing is certain: We cannot achieve good health without exercising. Regular physical activity is an essential key to being slim and healthy.

But—and here's the key point—with the regular use of Chitosan, you don't have to do tremendous amounts of exercise. Just keep doing a little more than you did yesterday. As we've said before, if you eat a *little* less, exercise a *little* more, and take Chitosan, you will lose weight and improve your health. You won't have to pant going up a flight of stairs, and hurrying to catch a bus won't make you feel as if your last hour had come. In other words, you can get yourself into pretty good shape, and with the help of Chitosan, you can not only do it without a major effort, you can get there and then actually stay that way.

Think of your weight as a reflection of the amount of calories you take in versus the amount you expend. It's like a bank: You deposit your paycheck, then you draw money out to pay the bills. What bills does the body have to pay? Well, it has to pay to run the basal metabolism, to move muscles, and to go through all of the processes involved in breaking down and absorbing food.

Basal metabolism represents the calories the body burns just to stay alive. The body is like a factory that employs billions of workers—our cells. Each one of these workers is constantly performing its designated duties and burning up fuel while doing so. It takes a surprising number of calories just to keep the factory going, to keep our hearts beating, our lungs inhaling and exhaling air, our temperatures stable, our nerves and hormones in working order. In fact, it can take as much as 70 percent of a normal day's caloric intake just to stay alive!

The amount of calories needed just to keep the body alive is called the basal metabolic rate, or BMR for short. The BMR is influenced by several things. Usually, the younger we are, the higher the BMR and the faster we burn calories. Tall people generally have higher BMRs than short people, and those with greater amounts of muscle have higher rates than those with greater amounts of fat. Because men tend to be taller and more muscular than women, they also have higher BMRs than women.

Fevers, stress, and overactive thyroids cause the BMR to soar, while fasting makes it plummet. The best way to increase your basal metabolic rate is to exercise. That does 2 things: It tends to speed up our metabolism (in a sense, it makes us younger), and it increases muscle mass. The best way to decrease BMR is to fast or go on a starvation diet. Doing so makes your body think it needs to shift into a lower gear and burn calories as slowly as possible.

Food assimilation, which involves breaking down the food you eat and absorbing it into your body, also burns up calories. The muscles of the esophagus and digestive tract contract to send the food on its way through yards of intestines, cells secrete enzymes and special juices to break the food into simpler substances that can be absorbed; other cells take up these substances and send them off through the bloodstream to their destinations. All of these tasks take energy. Just as it takes money to make money, it takes calories to burn calories. In fact, the mere presence of food in the digestive tract speeds up the overall metabolism.

The third way that the body burns energy is through physical activity and exercise. Although this accounts for only about 30 percent of the average person's energy expenditure, it can make a big difference in body weight. During physical activity, energy is expended moving the muscles, speeding up the heart rate, and increasing respiration. The more energy the muscles exert and the greater the length of time they do so, the more calories are burned and the larger the muscles become. As a side benefit, the more muscle tissue you develop, the faster your BMR becomes.

Your body pays these bills with the energy you deposit in the form of food (sort of an energy paycheck). To lose weight, you must pay out more in bills than you deposit with your paycheck. This forces you to dip into your savings account (your fat stores) in order to pay the bills. So the dieter has choices: Take in less energy, pay out more energy, or preferably, do both.

Why Can't I Lose Weight Permanently Without Exercise?

Most people who have a weight problem aren't just overeaters. Like Debbie, they may also have slow basal metabolic rates. A slow BMR can be the result of genetics, restrictive dieting that made the body believe it was starving, or a lack of muscle mass. No matter what the reason, the only healthy and effective way to speed up your BMR is to exercise, which builds muscle tissue. And the only way to do that is to get moving! But don't worry about a lifetime of drudgery. First of all, you're not trying to lose weight merely by speeding up your BMR. That's an important additional boost to help you along. The basic thing you are doing is reducing your caloric intake, which you have already done with Chitosan and the healthy eating habits we have discussed.

In fact, one important reason to exercise more once you start losing weight and assimilating less fat, is that your body is carrying less of a burden and so actually doing less work. That could result in its burning fewer calories—and in your not losing further weight, even with Chitosan.

So, you do need to do at least enough extra exercise to compensate. And it would be nice to do just a little more than that.

What Else Can Exercise Do for Me?

Besides increasing your BMR, exercise helps ensure that your body breaks down fat instead of muscle as you lose weight. When the amount of food you take doesn't provide enough energy to pay the bills, your body dips into its own energy stores. It will tend to break down fat first because that's where it stores the extra energy it needs for hard times (which, in our modern world, rarely come). But it can also take apart some muscle tissue in order to get the calories that it needs to keep going. This will not be a major problem if you follow the program, but you want to avoid making it even a minor problem by preserving as much muscle tissue as you can. The more muscle tissue you have, the higher your BMR and the more likely you are to be fit. The only way to preserve muscle tissue is to exercise to at least a reasonable degree. The reason you don't need much exercise to preserve your muscle mass is that whatever mass you now have, be it that of Arnold Schwarzenegger in his prime or a typical couch potato, you have achieved it as the result of the exercise you now do. If you increase that level—even if the increase only goes from almost none to very little—you will increase your muscle mass to some extent. Having said that, however, now let me emphasize that within reasonable limits (ah, there's that phrase again!) more exercise is always better than less.

So, let's take a look at some of the wonderful things that exercise can do for you and your body.

1. Increase the basal metabolic rate, allowing you to burn calories faster.
2. Preserve and build muscle tissue, preventing it from being depleted by the body for use as energy.
3. Lower body fat stores.
4. Develop and increase physical strength.
5. Contribute to a faster, steadier, more permanent weight loss.
6. Strengthen your heart and circulation.
7. Increase your energy and endurance.
8. Improve your sleep.
9. Improve your sex drive.
10. Improve your appearance.
11. Help regulate your bodily functions, such as digestion and elimination.
12. Reduce stress.
13. Slow the onset of some of the signs and symptoms of aging.
14. Make all physical tasks easier to accomplish.
15. Contribute to a positive mental outlook and an improved sense of well-being.
16. Help control high blood pressure.
17. Help control blood cholesterol.
18. Help control diabetes.
19. Help prevent osteoporosis.
20. Help ease the pain of osteoarthritis.
21. Lower blood fats.

22. Increase levels of growth hormone, which in turn can help tone your muscles and help you look and feel more youthful.

The good news is that you can get all of these benefits without putting yourself on a terribly rigorous training schedule or spending 3 hours a day at the gym. All you really need to do is exercise moderately for 30 minutes a day, 4 times a week. You will get a benefit if you do less exercise than that—as long as it's more than you did before. But you will get the full impact if you achieve that minimum. That's a pretty small investment for such a large return.

The Elements of a Good Exercise Program

Probably the single most important factor in a successful exercise program is identifying the kind of activity that you'll actually do. Joining a fancy gym or purchasing all the latest running gear isn't going to do anything for you if you give up after 3 weeks and go back to being a couch potato. So, first find something that you love.

Now, of course, here's the problem: Many of us simply don't enjoy any form of exercise. Fine, if that's you, you'll have trouble with reaching an optimum exercise level. But, remember, it doesn't matter. You will still lose weight and improve your health as long as you do a little more exercise than you did before.

On the other hand, many people who say they hate to exercise are casting their net too narrowly. Do you hate to ski, bicycle, run around playing touch football with your 10-year-old, play tag with your grandchildren or squash with a friend? Do you really hate walking briskly on the beach at sunset? Do you . . . well, you get the idea. Any of these activities, and dozens more, are an excellent way to reach the ideal training objective of at least half an hour a day, 4 days a week.

A 37-year-old patient of mine named Jeannine told me that

she had always been enamored of the ballet, even as a little girl. But it wasn't until the age of 20 that she took her first lesson. "That first year of ballet lessons was hard. Even though I went to class 3 times a week, I always felt like such a klutz. I couldn't do anything and everything hurt." But one day, after about a year, the teacher asked Jeannine to demonstrate a certain step to a new student. "I was so shocked. I thought, 'She thinks I can do this!'" After that, Jeannine was asked to join the intermediate ballet class. Today she has 17 years' worth of ballet classes under her belt, and although she will never be a professional dancer, she has reaped tremendous rewards from her effort. She has the strong, firm body and the good health of someone 15 years her junior. She thinks of ballet class as "taking a break from the world."

"Ballet has been so wonderful for me, physically, mentally, and even spiritually. And it doesn't even feel like exercising. I spend so much time focusing on the artistic side of it, on doing a step perfectly and beautifully, that I don't even think about the fact that I'm moving my muscles." Jeannine plans to dance for the rest of her life. "I just can't imagine giving it up," she says.

Jeannine found the key to lifelong fitness: She fell in love with a form of exercise. She had to work at it, especially in the beginning, and she took a bit of a risk by starting that quickly. She might have given up before she ever really got going—beginning a bit more slowly would have worked just as well and wouldn't have been as tough. But with perseverance she overcame her temporary stumbling block. And so can you.

Go to the gym, if that's what you think you'll enjoy. But if not, look for something else. Perhaps you'd enjoy country and western dancing. Try it once. Or maybe you'll get an idea by watching the sports channels, reading fitness magazines, or talking to your friends. With luck, you'll find an activity you love. It may be as common as jogging or as exciting as fencing, as beautiful as ballet or as warlike as karate. Or you may decide to indulge in a variety of different exercises: a tennis game on Monday, a brisk walk on Tuesday, a day off on Wednesday, chopping wood on Thursday, a workout at the gym on Friday, and romping with the kids on the weekend. There, that's more exercise than you need!

Whatever you choose, if you decide to try for a full exercise program there are 3 things that need to be figured into your program: frequency, intensity, and time.

FREQUENCY

For the best results, you should do some form of exercise at least 4 times per week. It needn't be too strenuous, or take up too much of your day. And even on your off days, it helps if you do something physical. The important thing is to keep moving.

At the start, if you haven't been doing any exercise, you will find that 4 times a week is simply too much. Don't push it. Work out once or twice a week. Skip a day or 2 if you find the whole thing too tedious, and then go back to it a day or 2 later, rested and with renewed enthusiasm. It's not so bad if you miss a little exercise because you're taking the Chitosan and losing weight.

The fact is that as time passes and you continue to lose weight (or keep it down) without your normal, terrible—and doomed—dieting efforts, you'll find your energy level creeping up. Very gradually, you'll find that exercise is a little easier, a little more fun. You'll do more.

At this point, you see a very happy upward spiral starting to form. The more you exercise, the more you'll find you want to exercise. People who are fit will tell you that after a day or two of little physical activity, the urge to exercise can become overwhelming. They've just got to get out and do something! The same can be true for you.

But, I repeat, don't push for it. Just find yourself something physical you enjoy, and then do it as frequently as you can without having to force yourself unduly. For most people, this gradual approach will lead to doing more and more exercise over time—and feeling better and better about it. You never know: While you're not looking, you just might become a real athlete.

INTENSITY

Aerobic exercise includes any exercise performed at a rate that puts a consistent demand on the cardiovascular system. You breathe harder and your heart rate speeds up during aerobic activities, conditioning not only muscles but your heart and lungs as well. One great advantage to aerobic exercise is that the well-conditioned muscles it produces become more likely to burn fat as fuel instead of glucose.

But wait a minute. I am only suggesting that you place a *slightly* higher demand on your body than you normally do. You should become warm, not bright red, in the face. Your breathing should speed up but stop short of heavy panting. Your pulse and heartbeat should speed up, but not to the pounding level. Enjoy what you're doing; don't try to kill yourself.

Aerobic means with oxygen, and any activity that increases your intake of oxygen and your heart rate can be considered aerobic exercise. (Bicycling, swimming, jogging, circuit weight training, and other forms of sustained movement that involve the large muscle groups can all be aerobic exercises, if done properly.)

For maximum efficiency, your heart should be beating fast enough to be in your particular target zone and has to keep beating that fast throughout your aerobic workout.

Before we look at the target range numbers, find your pulse. Look at the underside of either wrist, just below the thumb side of the palm. A prominent tendon runs down the middle of your lower arm, slightly off-center, toward the thumb. Place your first and second fingers on the thumb side of this tendon and press slightly. You should feel a slight throbbing; that's your pulse. To figure your heartbeats per minute, count the beats of your pulse for 6 seconds and then multiply by 10. (A watch with a second hand is necessary.)

To make sure you're exercising aerobically, stop and take your pulse during your workout. It should fall somewhere within the target zone that's appropriate for your age. However, while this is worth checking on the table below, what is more important is that your exercise feels good. If you are in pain, panting, feeling nauseous, perspiring excessively, or just not enjoying the effort, slow down; you're working too hard. The concept of no pain, no gain has done more harm to exercise than anything I can think of. Pain is aversive and is likely to cause you to hate exercising—and therefore stop doing it. Gain comes from exercising regularly because you enjoy it. (Of course, professional athletes, serious competitors, and the like do have to suffer to achieve their goals. But that comes with the territory, and apparently they kind of like it. In any case, that sort of rigor is only appropriate for winning in a competitive arena. It has nothing much in common with the exercise that is right for you to lose weight and live healthily.)

Pulse Rates During Aerobic Exercise

Age	Target Zone
20	120–150
25	117–146
30	114–142
35	111–138
40	108–135
45	105–131
50	102–127
55	99–123
60	96–120
65	93–116
70	90–113

There's a simple way to eyeball whether or not you're in your zone without using a stopwatch, or stopping to check your pulse. It's called the talk-sing test. Suppose you and your exercise friend want to know if you're walking briskly enough. If you can talk with your friend as you're walking along but you can't sing to her (without getting out of breath), you're probably moving along at a pretty good pace. (Singing takes more breath than talking so if you can sing, you're not working hard enough!)

TIME

If the sort of exercise you are planning to do involves truly vigorous bursts of energy, you should spend 5–10 minutes warming up your muscles. The best warm-up exercises are *gently* aerobic: jumping jacks, jogging in place, bicycling, or anything else that gets your blood moving. Start slowly, easing your body into high gear. Just as you wouldn't start a cold car, slam it into gear, and then roar down the street at 60 miles per hour, you don't want to leap right into your exercise routine.

Also, as part of your warm-up, you should do some stretching exercises. Again, start gradually and work your way up to a full stretch.

To achieve maximum effectiveness (especially if you are seeking to become competitively fit) your total exercise session should last at least 30 minutes for maximum fat-burning and cardiovascular-strengthening effects. Obviously, if you are in training for a particular sport, you may need much more time than this. No one can compete in a marathon by training for only half an hour a day! But athletic training is not the subject of this book; I am talking merely about weight loss and healthy living. For that, you do need to exercise. As I have emphasized before, all increases in your exercise program are helpful if you are also eating a little less and taking Chitosan. However, for optimum fat burning, your exercise sessions should last for at least half an hour. Some patients ask me why 30 minutes is the magic number for burning fat. Why not 3 separate 10 minute sessions?

During times of intensive exercise involving a short burst of intense energy (for example, while dashing 100 yards or lifting a heavy weight), the muscles primarily use glucose for fuel. But if the exercise continues at a lower intensity for some time (as it does in swimming, walking, or jogging) the body eventually switches to fat as its primary fuel. Aerobic exercise encourages the switch because it provides the muscles with oxygen, which is essential in the fat-burning process. However, before the switch occurs there is a time gap while your body decides whether the exercise counts as a short burst or as an extended, fat-burning effort. Most experts today feel that this gap may be anywhere from 5 to 15 minutes. Thereafter, the body burns fat. I believe that 30 minutes is a reasonable minimum time for exercise to continue and for a meaningful amount of fat to be used up—although 45 minutes or even longer is better, *provided* you enjoy it enough to be able to work out that consistently.

However gradually you start increasing your exercise, your efforts will almost certainly gain momentum. As time passes and you decrease your food intake—partly by cutting down and partly by taking Chitosan—your energy level naturally rises and you become more active. And that makes longer and more vigorous aerobic effort both easier and more enjoyable. You slowly get hooked on one of the few addictions that is good for you.

But there is more good news to come. It is that once aerobic exercise has become a regular part of your life, its benefits just seem to snowball. The more aerobic exercise you do, the more efficiently your body will burn fat. (That's because it becomes better at delivering oxygen to the muscles. The presence of oxygen makes it possible to use fat as a fuel source.) So, in effect, you can turn your body into a fat-burning machine just by exercising aerobically 3–4 times a week. And soon you won't just be burning fat only during exercise sessions—you'll be burning some fat *all* the time.

When you've completed your aerobic exercising, it's important that you always do a short cool-down. You don't want to get your heart going at its peak rate, then suddenly stop dead and go sit down. Instead, you should gradually bring your heart rate back down to its resting level. You can do a cool-down by performing a scaled-down version of your main exercise. (For example, if you've been jogging, jog very slowly in place.) Walking at a moderate pace is a good cool-down exercise. You'll also find that the cool-down is an excellent time to stretch more vigorously to help you stay limber all day (which, in turn, will make you more likely to move around more—and so burn off more calories). Your muscles, now warm, will be much less likely to strain or tear.

Caution: Before you begin any new exercise program, see your physician to discuss any health concerns you may have, especially if you are over 35 or have heart trouble, high blood pressure, any other health problems, concerns, or risk factors. And consider these tips:

+ Don't overdo it, especially at the beginning. Start slowly, increasing the intensity, time, or number of repetitions gradually over a period of weeks or months. Overdoing it can lead to injuries. If you injure yourself, you'll be more likely to abandon the program for good. Less dramatically, but just as bad for your long-term health, overexertion at the start can teach you that exercise is painful and unpleasant (which it doesn't have to be) and can convince you not to do any.

+ Expect to feel a little tired, out of breath, or slightly sore at first. But again I emphasize that these symptoms should be minor. Remember, your initial objective is to do a *little* more exercise, partly to make absolutely certain that you are not falling into the trap of doing less (perhaps because you have less weight to cart around), and partly because even a little bit of extra exercise will speed up your BMR and help you lose weight and get into shape faster. In any case, even if you inadvertently overdo it slightly at the start, don't worry. That's normal. Soon, your body will respond to the exercise, quickly learning to tolerate greater amounts of exercise. It's amazing what the human body can do in a brief period of time.

+ Stay with it. Try to exercise at least 4 days a week. Frequency and consistency are more important than quantity when it comes to exercise—especially if you are just starting out. As the ancient Greek philosopher Aristotle pointed out, "We are what we repeatedly do. Excellence, then, is not an act, but a habit." Your consistent effort will pay off, sooner than you think. Gradually, if you remain steady, the amount of exercise you do will increase. Within a few months, people will say to you, "I don't know how you do it. I certainly couldn't." Take the compliment, even though you and I both know that, with just a *little* effort—and Chitosan—your admirer could do just as well.

+ Keep breathing as you exercise. You need plenty of oxygen, especially during aerobic exercise. Holding your breath can defeat your purpose, raise your blood pressure, and prompt increased muscle soreness.

+ Tune in to your body's signals. Learn to distinguish between the mild pain of exerting unused muscles and the true pain of injury. If you feel dizzy, short of breath, tight-chested, or nauseated, stop and immediately see your doctor. In fact, if you occasionally reach the point where you just don't feel like continuing, pack up and go home. Better to miss one day of exercise than to put yourself into such a negative frame of mind about the whole thing that you give up exercising altogether.

The Best Kind of Exercise

The best kind of exercise is the one that you'll do. So pick a form of exercise (or a combination of several) and establish a regular routine that will fit into your lifestyle. But remember: Take it easy, especially if you haven't exercised in a while. Many, many people start out with boundless enthusiasm, doing too much too fast. Pushing too hard right from the start, they quickly become injured, exhausted, or just plain burned out.

Now that you know what exercise can do for you and what makes up a good exercise program, let's take a look at some of the different forms of exercise that might be right for you.

Walking

Walking is one of the easiest and most convenient of all forms of exercise. It requires no equipment other than a good pair of walking shoes and some comfortable clothing, and it can be done almost anywhere. It doesn't even demand good weather. In many areas of the country where snow and low temperatures are common, mall walking has become a great sport. And for years walkers have been eating up miles and miles worth of pavement in the comfort of their own homes by using treadmills. So for many people, especially former nonexercisers, walking is the sport of choice.

One of the best things about walking is that you can incorporate it into your daily routine pretty seamlessly. For example, you could walk instead of driving to work. You could take the dog out for a walk, which it would love, instead of sending it outside by itself. A friend of mine had his golden retriever trained to go for a run every evening when he returned from work. If he got home and didn't want to go jogging, the dog would drive him nuts until he did. "We used to run 3 miles every evening," my friend told me. "I would run 1 mile and the dog would run 2!"

Walking, at any pace, is better than sitting, but in order to get cardiovascular benefits you must do more than just stroll. Walking briskly can be just as effective as running or bicycling the same distance—it just takes longer. For starters, take yourself out for a walk around your neighborhood. Before you go, do 5 minutes worth of jumping jacks or pushups to warm up, or walk at a slow pace for the first few minutes. Then begin walking briskly. Make sure you keep up a good pace (see the talk-sing test above) and walk for as long as you care to. Try to do a little more each day. And try to find interesting places to walk. (Many cities have walking guides or books that will suggest good walks.) After a while, you'll forget about how long you've been walking, lost in the interest or beauty of your surroundings. Soon, 30 minutes will seem wholly insufficient.

As you come to the end of your walk, slow down to a strolling pace for 5 more minutes, finally finishing your workout with some stretches. Do this walking routine at least 4 times a week for the next few weeks. Once you find that it's easy for you to keep going for a half hour or more and you're feeling fine, move up to the next level, wogging.

Wogging

Wogging is my term for the combination of two of the best heart-strengthening exercises ever—walking and jogging. When wogging, walk for a block, then jog for a block. This greatly increases the intensity of the walking workout, as well as its cardiovascular benefits and calorie-burning power. Begin your wogging program with the same warm-ups used for the walking program. And, as I say about every one of my recommendations in this book, take it easy. For instance, in the beginning, you may want to walk 3 blocks and jog 1, gradually working up to a 1-to-1 ratio. When you've finished your session, always remember to cool down.

Of course, jogging is not for everybody. If you have some physical problem or just don't like doing it, choose something else. How about horseback riding, or beach volleyball, or playing table tennis flat out against a tough opponent. However, if you do like running, wogging is the perfect way to get in shape at the outset.

Jogging and Running

Jogging (a slow-paced run) and running are excellent ways to strengthen your heart and lungs, burn calories, increase muscle tone, and strengthen bones and joints while stepping up overall fitness. One of the most important keys to successful jogging or running is laying the proper groundwork. You need to build your body up gradually to the point where you can jog or run at a comfortable pace for at least 30 minutes. Unless you're already in great shape, or you have a true masochist's desire for pain, don't start by jogging for 30 minutes. Instead, work up to it. Like the song says, "Nice and easy does it every time!"

So before you begin to jog or run, lay the groundwork.

+ Begin with a program of walking at a pace that's slightly faster than a stroll. Do this at least 4 times a week for 45 minutes until you can do it easily.

+ Then walk briskly for 30 to 45 minutes at a time, until you can also do that easily.

+ Begin wogging. Walk briskly, then jog every third or fourth block.

+ Step up your wogging. Work up to walking 1 block, jogging the next, and so forth.

+ When jogging every other block becomes comfortable, begin to jog 2 blocks and walk 1, adding more jogging until you are jogging all the time. Keep it at a comfortable pace; don't push too hard.

+ Eventually, you may want to increase your pace and begin to run. Your body should be your guide. Don't overdo it.

When you've built up your endurance and wind, you should be able to jog 4–5 miles an hour (that's a 12–15–minute-mile pace). If you run, you should be able to move along at a 7–10 miles-per-hour pace.

A reminder here. It is a great feeling to be in excellent shape, the sort of shape that lets you run for half an hour without being seriously tired or even out of breath. I recommend the feeling—and the activity—to everyone. But it is not essential to feel this good. You can lose weight, reduce your fat retention, and lower your cholesterol (although probably not quite as much without vigorous exercise) by doing a little exercise, eating a little less, and using Chitosan. However—and this is my key point—once you start out on my Fat Blocker Program, you will find that you *want* to exercise. So, all I'm really trying to persuade you to do is to get started. The more vigorous, ideal effort will follow naturally, whether you are pushing for it or not. In fact, it will probably happen sooner if you are *not* pushing.

Pool Exercises

Exercising in the water has become quite popular in recent years with those who have joint pain, injuries, trouble keeping their balance, or who just plain love being in the water. The water provides resistance so your muscles have to work, but being in the pool eliminates the gravitational stress of exercising on land. Thus, your joints take less of a beating. And just about any kind of exercise can be done in the water: aerobic, strengthening, and/or stretching.

Don't shy away from water exercises if you aren't an expert swimmer or if you have trouble treading water for long periods of time. Most exercises can be done in the shallow end of the pool or with the use of a flotation device. And the benefits can be tremendous. Pool exercise:

+ Provides a form of exercise for those who have joint problems or weak muscles and might otherwise shun activity.

+ Supports the body during exercise, reducing the possibility of muscle strain or wear and tear on the joints.

+ Generally has the heart beating at a lower rate than it would while exercising on land, so greater amounts of activity can be tolerated at a higher intensity.

+ Can often be continued even when the exerciser has been injured. (Injured runners often train by "running" in the water while their injuries heal.)

+ Can help to relax muscles and ease pain.

✦ Reduces the possibility of overheating (because the water is usually cool).

Most of the exercises that you might do in aerobics class can be modified for use in the pool. An especially effective, calorie-burning exercise is water walking, or striding through thigh-deep or deeper water. The deeper the water, the better the workout because it takes more effort. And if you swing your arms, you're also working out your upper body. Try it in different directions—backwards, forwards, sideways, and diagonally. Remember that the need for the warm-up and cool-down applies to all forms of exercise that you do. But of course the length of exercise will vary. It's much easier to walk for 30 minutes on land than in the water! On the other hand, to reach your optimum fat-burning level, the ideal to keep in mind (your distant beacon) is that you should continue your cardiovascular effort for at least half an hour. Fine. So do 10 minutes in the water, and then 20 minutes jogging. You could even split the jogging in 2 and do 10 minutes in the water, 10 on solid ground, and then the last 10 minutes on your bicycle. (I call that a 30-minute Iron Man!)

Swimming

Swimming provides one of the best general body workouts that you can get because it involves the muscles of the legs, hips, midsection, shoulders, arms, and neck. All of these muscle groups are strengthened as they work against the resistance of the water. Simultaneously, the range of motion and flexibility of the joints is improved. Swimming steadily is also one of the best fat-burning activities, as it provides the aerobic benefits of cardiovascular strength, calorie expenditure, and an increased basal metabolic rate.

Like other pool exercises, swimming has the built-in benefits of body support, lack of joint stress and strain, and a cooling, refreshing environment in which to exercise. The only drawbacks are that you have to know how to swim, it doesn't provide the weight-bearing exercise that you need to maintain bone strength, and it gets your hair wet! Oh, and you do need a pool, lake, or ocean near at hand. These problems aren't impossible to solve, though. Swimming classes are offered at many YMCAs, YWCAs, and public pools. To maintain bone strength, you can walk or jog on the days that you don't swim or on the way to the pool. As for the wet hair, well, it will probably dry on your way back from the pool! Seriously, if you like swimming, it's well worth the time and effort to get involved.

Cycling

Riding a bicycle is a great aerobic exercise that gives your calves, thighs, gluteus maximus, and cardiovascular system a good workout without putting undue stress or strain on your hip, knee, or ankle joints. It can also provide you with lots of fresh air and interesting scenery (unless you're on a stationary bike). The drawbacks are that it does very little for upper-body strength, and like swimming it is not a weight-bearing exercise so it doesn't help stimulate bone strength and density.

As with all exercises, you should start slowly. Cycle at a moderate pace on relatively flat ground. Gradually increase your speed over time, until you're averaging 70–90 pedal revolutions per minute (i.e., 70 downstrokes of your right foot per minute).

Stationary cycling is a good way to get a quick aerobic workout. But no matter what kind of cycling you do, consider these tips:

+ Warm up for 5–10 minutes before adding resistance to your stationary bike workout or climbing hills in your cycling route.

+ Make sure the seat is at the proper height so that your knee is still somewhat bent when your foot is at the bottom of the pedal revolution.

✦ Make sure that you're cycling in the proper gear. A gear that's too high will strain your knees.

✦ When cycling outdoors, always wear a helmet and never wear headphones. (You need to be able to hear an approaching car.)

Aerobics and Other Kinds of Exercise

Walking, wogging, jogging, running, swimming, or cycling aren't the only kinds of aerobic exercise. Any physical activity that gets and keeps your heart rate up and your breath coming faster qualifies as aerobic. Doing heavy yard work, mowing the lawn, washing the car, vacuuming energetically, or chasing your kids around can provide you with aerobic exercise just as surely as running a mile does. And there is absolutely no need to do the same thing every time. After all, you don't eat the same things every day (except, of course, for Chitosan), so why should you do the same exercise? In fact, varying what you do has two major advantages: It converts exercising from chore to fun so you never get bored, and it ensures that all your muscles get a workout. The only important consideration is to do some form of aerobic activity for at least 30 consecutive minutes at least 4 to 5 times a week. The closer you get to that goal, the better you'll feel.

When you do start exercising (gently at first, remember), make a real effort to find stimulating activities. For instance, many people enjoy the stimulation and encouragement they find in an aerobics class with inspiring instructors. The energy in these classes can be contagious, while the friendships that spring up make going to class even more fun. The exercises are usually done to the beat of high-energy music, and low-impact formats offer protection against joint wear and tear.

Other activities that can provide aerobic benefits and overall physical fitness include cross-country skiing, rowing, tennis, circuit-weight training (without long breaks between weights), and just about any sport that involves steady, continuous moving. Once again, let me remind you: It doesn't matter *which* aerobic exercise you do as long as you do it, you do it regularly, and it keeps your heart beating in the target zone for the required amount of time.

For the more aesthetically inclined, jazz dance or ballet classes may be just the thing, and many dance studios cater to adults who are just beginning to learn to dance. Dancing brings strength, flexibility, and balance that can put a willing participant on the road to physical fitness, weight loss, and a new appreciation of the human form. Again, the advantage of being part of a group should not be underestimated. It is a lot more encouraging to hear your friends say, "We missed you," than to listen to your spouse nagging you because you missed going to your class again.

In the end, you see, it doesn't matter what sport or exercise you do, or even how much you do at the beginning. Once you get started on the Fat Blocker Program, including at least *some* additional exercise, your physical energy will gradually increase, and so will the time and energy you *want* to expend on exercise.

Once you get started, you'll find yourself in a classic vicious circle. The more you do, the more you have to do. But, for once, it isn't vicious. It's wonderful! By eating sensibly and a little less than before, starting to exercise (or slightly and gradually stepping up the exercise you did before), and taking Chitosan, you will slowly but surely find yourself moving towards the exercise ideal. After a while, you will find yourself to be in better shape than ever before. In the words of one of my patients—and the thought has been expressed by many others—"I've never been this fit in my whole, long life!"

It's really so clear. Keep eating less, exercising a little more, and taking Chitosan. As you start to make exercise a regular part of your life, you'll get hooked on it. Nothing else can make you feel quite so young, alive, and full of energy.

9

◆

Staying Motivated to Lose Weight

"The entire world is conspiring against me, Dr. Fox, the entire world." That's how 34-year-old Barbara began our conversation when she came to my office one day. Plopping down in the chair in disgust, the 170-pound, 5' 4" mother of 3 continued, "I'm trying to watch my weight, I'm trying to change my eating habits, but I can't. My kids are always wolfing down Sugar Pops, cupcakes, and red licorice, all at the same time. They eat in front of me, they leave it on the table, the boxes are in the cupboard. At work, someone's always bringing in glazed doughnuts. At lunchtime, the menu is full of main dishes with Alfredo in the name, and then there's nothing to eat but cookies and soda in the afternoon."

I thought I might interject a suggestion while Barbara took a breath, but she continued before I had a chance. "Then, at home, I'm in charge of the cooking! I've got to see all that food, I've got to handle it, I've got to smell it while it's cooking. And I'm starving while I'm seeing it, handling it, and smelling it. And then, the TV advertises nothing but food, food, food! How can I avoid all of these temptations? It's a conspiracy!"

Of course, Barbara is right. It's almost impossible not be be exposed to food—and wonderful-tasting food at that. McDonald's, Burger King, and Pizza Hut; Nabisco, General Mills, and Kraft; Miller, Budweiser, Coca-Cola, and Pepsi; 10,000 restaurant chefs and millions of well-meaning mothers spend half their working hours figuring out how to seduce us into eating more. We seem almost powerless to resist.

Moreover, our so-called lack of willpower is not that at all. The true fact is that we are evolutionarily programmed not to resist the blandishments of food. The real reason that we cannot stay on a low-calorie, hunger-inducing diet for long is not that we lack mental fortitude but that to remain permanently hungry is, quite literally, against human nature. Not to mention uncomfortable!

Humans were programmed, way back in the era of prehistoric man (and quite possibly even before humans evolved from our australopithicine forebears), to eat more than they needed when food was abundant in order to have reserves when it was not. They stored the excess as fat and held onto it tenaciously for emergency use. In fact, our bodies are willing to part with certain fat reserves (such as those saddle bags on the upper thighs or the fatty bulges on the underside of the buttocks) only under two conditions: If we are close to starvation or, for pregnant women, if their fetus needs nourishment. Under few circumstance can we lose fat in those locations.

During our evolution, our survival depended on this mechanism of fat storage because periods of deprivation were inevitable. However, for most of us today, this fat-storage mechanism is not offset by frequent or even occasional lack-of-food emergencies. Inevitably, therefore, we have to fight and struggle to keep our weight down—and most of us fail, at least to some extent. Given our evolutionary programming, most of us simply cannot avoid gaining weight as we age.

Does that then lead to the inevitable conclusion that trying to lose weight (or maintain our optimum weight) as we age is futile? Well, while I wouldn't go that far, I must admit that it has been a huge problem up to now, and one that for most people has at best been only partly solved up to now. However, the situation has been altered drastically by the Chitosan program.

While there is still some difficulty involved in losing weight and keeping it off (because a certain amount of restraint is still needed, and restraint is not one of the things we humans are particularly good at), it is now well within reach and entirely practical for every healthy person.

It is in this context that I offer the following suggestions for how to motivate yourself to lose weight. You now know that with the help of Chitosan you definitely will be able to control your weight. And that knowledge itself is a powerful motivator. As one of my favorite aphorisms has it, your power flows where your attention goes.

Believing You Can

I am a great believer in using positive thinking in every aspect of life. In my 40-plus years as an internist and cardiologist, I've seen first hand how our thoughts have a profound impact on our physical health. Unfortunately, many of us have filled our minds with the kind of unhappy thoughts that invite disease by weakening the immune system. Millions of Americans are suffering from depression, anxiety, irritability, "hatred and hurted," and other emotional problems. These thoughts can actually change the body's chemistry and promote cancer, heart disease, immune system disorders, and many other diseases. I have no doubt that unhappy thoughts can also contribute to a slowed-down metabolism and obesity.

It helps to visualize something before doing it. That sets in your mind a picture of success, a goal to strive for. Sports psychologists do this when they teach their athletes to visualize the roar of victory that will emanate from the crowd as they touch the finish line first. At a

> Always keep your goals in the front of your mind. Constantly seeing yourself succeeding is the first step toward success. And often the most important step as well.

more common level, we do this constantly, every day, even though we may not be aware of it. We think, for example, "I need to take a drive," and we imagine getting our keys and wallets, getting into our cars, and driving along a mountain road. Only *then* do we actually get the keys and wallet, leave the house, and hop in the car. We *saw* it in our minds before we did it.

Visualizing a positive end result is a very effective way of achieving a goal. But some people have difficulty doing so, for their ability to visualize a goal depends on their belief in what they are visualizing. It is difficult, for example, for a runner who always loses and whose times are known to be worse than those of his competition to imagine himself winning races. He feels that he cannot possibly see himself winning unless there is a logical reason why previous history won't apply to the next race . . . perhaps a new training technique. So, rather than visualizing success, he sees himself losing. And that unhappy vision makes it even more difficult to triumph. Unhappy past experiences become self-fulfilling prophecies of future performance.

This is exactly what happens to many dieters. They "know" from bitter and repeated past experience that diets don't work. Therefore, instead of imagining themselves as slim and beautiful, they see themselves as even pudgier and more out of shape. They find it a lot easier to fantasize about eating a scrumptious toffee nut chocolate candy bar than a bunch of carrot sticks. Of course, with such unbidden images of candy bars and the like filling their imaginations—and without any counteracting images of ultimate success with which to fight back—the goodies become even more difficult to resist. Many of us can't.

But matters are wholly different once Chitosan is added to the mix. At last there is an entirely logical reason to believe we can lose weight. Indeed, there is no doubt that, with a degree of self-control well within our reach, we *can*. As a result, we can start visualizing positive weight-reduction scenarios without boggling our imaginations with their sheer impossibility. Now we have a reason—and therefore the tools—to convert our fantasy about Snickers bars into a more productive fantasy about luscious, juicy peaches, or fresh-baked bread, or. . . .

Best of all, however, we can now start to imagine food—good, healthy food, not the dry, diet food you really hate—in context with looking good and feeling healthy.

It may seem a little silly at first, but try the following visualization technique. Imagine yourself sitting down to a delicious, health-promoting meal. You're relaxed, feeling full of energy and well-being. See yourself eating this wonderful meal, savoring the flavors and aromas. With each bite you become slimmer, more attractive, and healthier. Repeat the fantasy every time a meal is approaching. Concentrate.

For many of my patients, the technique of imagining (or imaging, really) does work. Indeed, keeping these mental pictures firmly in our minds may be one of the most important keys to weight loss and good eating. Always remember: If you can *see* yourself eating healthfully, you can *do* it! To paraphrase words of Napoleon Hill, "Whatever the mind can conceive and believe, it can achieve!"

With Chitosan assisting us, it is easy to believe that we can eat healthily and lose weight. We *can* do it, we can maintain our appropriate weight, even if it sometimes seems as if the entire world is conspiring to get us to eat all the wrong foods for all the wrong reasons. But of course, potential pitfalls still await us. So let's examine them and see how we can easily avoid these traps.

Eating by Habit

We are all creatures of habit. Most of us probably have no idea just how much of what we do is in response to some external cue. We get up in response to the ringing of the alarm clock. We eat breakfast because it's 7:00 A.M. and that's breakfast time. We respond to thousands of cues as we drive to work, rarely thinking about any of them. We answer the phone, we shuffle papers, we sign our names, we go to lunch, we punch our time cards, we smile when we're introduced to others, we say "excuse me" after bumping into someone. All of this is simply habit. If our habits are generally good, we can get through life fairly easily. But what if they're bad? Then we risk reaping a bitter harvest, for habits are so much a part of our unconscious actions. We may suffer consequences for things we don't even know we're doing.

It used to be that every time I walked in the front door after a hard day's work, I'd head straight for the kitchen to grab some cookies and milk. It didn't matter if dinner was waiting on the stove, it didn't matter what time it was, it didn't even matter if I wasn't really hungry. That was my habit, I *had* to do it. Then one day I stopped by the house at 11 in the morning, right after a breakfast meeting. As usual, I headed straight for the cookie jar. But this time it hit me: Why was I eating cookies at 11:00 A.M., especially when I had just eaten a very large and filling breakfast? And was going to be having lunch soon? It was habit, pure and simple—and a bad one, at that!

Fortunately, habits (like rules) are made to be broken. Once you know you have a poor eating habit, you can probably break it easily enough. And how do you know? Well, one good way I suggest to my patients is to write down every bit of food they eat for a few days, even the tiniest morsel. They're often amazed to learn what they're eating. One lady was dumbfounded to discover how much cheese she was eating at night while watching television. "I never thought of the cheese as food," she protested. "It's just a comforter to help me sleep." But it was also almost pure fat.

If you find any surprising eating habits (as did my patient), think about just why you are eating in that way. Once you do so, the reason will probably be obvious. You will understand the emotional, situational, or other triggers that have you eating the wrong foods in the wrong amounts, at the wrong times, and for the wrong reasons.

Avoiding Emotional Triggers

An incredible amount of eating is triggered by anger, anxiety, depression, happiness, frustration, boredom, fatigue, and other emotional states. Food is a sort of instant fix, a way to dull the pain and make ourselves feel good. Unfortunately, this instant fix can turn into a long-term problem if it's overdone.

A 26-year-old woman named Jennifer came to see me because she was feeling weak and tired. When I asked her what was going on in her life, she replied, "My daughter died of leukemia, so I've been binge-eating, shoving down the equivalent of 3–4 meals at a time. I eat because it feels comforting. Then I realize I ate too much and don't want to get fat, so I throw up."

Jennifer's case was extreme, but she's not the only one to eat when she's unhappy. Ann, a 48-year-old woman I hadn't seen for a couple years, was red-faced when she came to my office. "I've gained 50 pounds, Dr. Fox," she said. "The problem is I feel so alone and unhappy since my divorce. I have this wonderful job in which I get praised all day long. Then I come home to my apartment and my cat. The phone never rings on the weekend. It never rings at all. I just eat and eat; it's the only thing that gives me satisfaction. It's also made me 50 pounds heavier."

We eat when we're unhappy, and we eat when we're happy. Weddings, graduations, birthday parties, confirmations, bar mitzvahs, promotions: We celebrate all our important life events and joys by eating. Joy is intimately associated with food.

But now that we've discovered the link between eating and emotions, we can plan alternatives. And where an alternative is either impractical or undesirable (after all, a slice of your daughter's wedding cake is more than a mere snack), you can compensate by taking extra Chitosan.

However, if you find that you're eating a package of cookies to make yourself feel better when you get angry, anxious, frustrated, or stressed out, try one of the following instead.

✦ Confront the problem or the problem person.

✦ Exercise. Go for a walk or a run, take a dance class, go to the gym and work out.

✦ Try relaxation techniques. Follow along with a relaxation tape, go to a yoga class, get a massage, meditate, lie down and take a nap.

✦ Forgive the person who has harmed you. Remember that forgiveness is a gift to yourself. If forgiving someone helps you avoid overeating and damaging your health, it's a very important gift indeed.

If boredom is the culprit that makes you eat:

✦ Keep your hands busy—clean out a cupboard or do a hands-on project.

✦ Visit a friend.

✦ See a movie.

Remember: Food is for satisfying physical, not emotional, hunger. Next time you get the urge to splurge, ask yourself, "Am I really hungry, or am I trying to make myself feel better for some other reason?"

Dealing With Situational Triggers

When I realized I was eating cookies just because I had entered my house, I decided to change my homecoming routine. Instead of heading straight to the kitchen, I went straight for the shower. A hot shower relaxed me and refreshed me much more than the cookies ever did.

Everybody has situational triggers. One of the most common is what I like to call monkey see, monkey do. This trigger has gotten to all of us. We walk into the coffee room at work. Everyone is standing around munching on doughnuts. Since everyone else is eating doughnuts, we start munching one, too. Or perhaps we go into the kitchen at home and our child is having a peanut butter sandwich. Suddenly, we feel as if we must have one, as well. Social gatherings especially encourage overeating. It's easy to eat compulsively when we're feeling nervous and ill at ease at a cocktail party. Eating gives us something to do.

Another common situational trigger is watching television. It's easy to shift into the automatic-eating mode when our minds are elsewhere. Have you ever noticed how much food you can pack away (without even noticing it) when you eat while watching TV? To make matters worse, we're exposed to countless food commercials that are themselves triggers for overeating. Plus, time spent sitting in front of the TV is time *not* spent participating in calorie-burning activities. No wonder a study done at Auburn University found that men who watched television for at least 3 hours a day were twice as likely to be obese than men who watched for less than an hour.

Just as I was able to break my cookies-and-milk habit by changing my routine once I walked through the front door, many of your situational triggers may be defused just by making a little change. Try and pinpoint what sets you off. Once you've figured out what, where, and when you eat, as well as your emotional state before and after eating, you can plan strategies to help you avoid these weight-loss land mines.

EATING WHILE COOKING

It's really hard not to taste the foods we cook. Sometimes, in fact, it's absolutely necessary. How else will we know if the seasoning is right, if the noodles are done, or the food is hot enough? But some cooks eat enough while standing over the pot to make up a whole meal! If this is your problem, try one of these strategies:

✦ Have a small snack (a piece of fruit or some cut-up vegetables) before you begin to cook so you won't be overly hungry.

✦ Never taste from the cooking spoon. (It's unsanitary, anyway!) Instead, take a sample from the pot with the cooking spoon and pour it into a small teaspoon. Taste from the teaspoon. This extra step may be enough trouble to make you stop and think before you taste.

EATING BECAUSE IT'S THERE

You've probably heard the old joke about a guy who went on a diet. He explained, "It's a seafood diet. I *see* food, I eat it!" To some extent, we're all on the see-food diet; we're programmed to be stimulated by the sight of food. That's one of the things that kept us alive back in prehistoric times. Unfortunately, in this day and age we see food all the time. We're bombarded with visual stimuli that encourage us to eat when we don't need to, or even want to. Here are a few tips to help you cope with the visual cues:

✦ In addition to keeping your Chitosan bag with you at all times, put some low-calorie munchies and healthy snacks such as carrot sticks and fresh fruit in the front of your refrigerator.

✦ Use a small plate rather than a large one so that your portions will *look* big but won't *be* big. (I realize that this may seem hokey, but it works for two reasons: It really does make the food you're about to eat look more satisfying, and remember what you *believe* is half of what *is;* and in addition, just the slightly unusual act of choosing a smaller plate will remind you not to eat more than you want.)

✦ Serve food from the stove top, rather than in large bowls on the table (family style). That way you won't see the extra food while you're eating. It also takes more effort to get up from the table to get another serving.

✦ Bring healthy snacks (your Chitosan bag) to work and set them on your desk. After eating these healthy foods, you won't be so tempted to gobble high-calorie snacks.

✦ Only eat in certain designated rooms at home, for example, the kitchen and the dining room. That way you reduce the number of places at home that you associate with eating. After a while, eating will not be directly on your mind as you sit down in the den to watch television.

✦ Keep high-calorie foods out of sight and out of mind.

✦ Better yet, bring only healthful, low-calorie food into the house. If you don't buy fried pork rinds or triple-chocolate tortes in the first place, they won't be there to tempt you.

✦ Make main dishes in advance and freeze them in individual portions. Or, keep on hand a supply of some of the excellent new, calorie-controlled frozen meals. Either way, you'll have the right meal size available when you come home hungry. Just pop it into the microwave! But remember, don't make the portions too small. If you are not satisfied with your single-serve portion, you'll probably just grab a second one. And if you're like me, you'll certainly polish it off entirely. Instead of a portion of maybe a third more than your prepared meal (which would have satisfied you nicely), you have now tricked yourself into eating twice as much as you started out to consume.

EATING ON THE RUN

Our lives have become super fast paced in recent years. We often don't have time to sit down as a family to a leisurely dinner. That's a sad fact of modern life, and some of us may be suffering both physically and psychologically because of it. Of course, others may enjoy the challenge of the fast pace—but even so, they probably aren't helping their physical well-being. For one thing, we all tend to eat more junk when we're forced to grab something quickly. Still, it *is* possible to eat well, even when you are eating on the run:

✦ No matter how rushed you are, when it's time to eat a meal, always try to stop what you're doing, even for a moment, to sit down and focus on what you're eating. It really doesn't take that long to eat a meal, especially if you're by yourself. You really *can* afford to take the time. You owe it to yourself to take that time because if you let eating become just one more of the 10 things you're doing at once, you'll end up eating more and feeling less satisfied. So don't talk on the phone, drive, do paperwork, read, or stand in front of the refrigerator while eating. Sit down and make every meal an occasion, even if for only 10 minutes.

In this respect, Chitosan can help because you have to think about it before you eat. How much fat does the meal you are about to eat contain, and therefore how much Chitosan should you be taking in advance of it? The very fact of such a decision will help remove the meal from merely one of your many concurrent activities and make it slightly special.

✦ Brown-bag it as much as possible. Fresh fruit, raw vegetables, nonfat yogurt, whole wheat bread, and nonfat cottage cheese are all easy to take along. They are also packed with nutrients. When you've got these good foods handy, you won't be forced to grab whatever is available. Since you should already be making your Chitosan bag into a habit, the extra effort of completing the meal may be something you can live with.

✦ If you do have to buy something to eat on the fly, consider dropping by the grocery store to pick up fresh produce or other nutritious food. Convenience stores also have fruit, juice, cut-up vegetables, bagels (but don't add globs of cream cheese!), dairy products, and other things that can keep you on the plan. Moreover, since nearly all such foods are now labeled with their fat content, you will know precisely what amount of fat your Chitosan has to deal with. Many fast-food restaurants have heart-healthy choices like grilled chicken sandwiches or baked potatoes, plain or with low-fat toppings.

EATING SOCIALLY

Eating at a social event, at parties, buffets, and other people's homes can really test our commitment to health. For starters, we can't control what kinds of foods are served or how they are prepared. We also can't control the portion size unless the food is served buffet style. And there are usually loads of high-fat, high-calorie goodies we may love but would prefer to avoid. This is when Chitosan can be a real lifesaver. By taking a dose 30 minutes before we plan to eat, we can indulge in *some* of those forbidden but delicious foods without having to pay the price in weight gain or poor health later on! Of course, the best course of all is to simply avoid the high-fat foods.

The Right Way to Use Chitosan

Your success on the Fat Blocker Program with Chitosan is, of course, ultimately dependent on your attitude toward yourself, toward building healthful eating habits that will last a lifetime, and toward the measured use of Chitosan. If you think that this supplement is a sort of license to overeat, you'll be very disappointed in the results. What it is, rather, is a license to eat correctly, a license to maintain your appropriate weight, a license to be healthy. If you abuse your body by taking handfuls of Chitosan and then gorging on high-calorie treats, you will end up gaining weight. (Remember: Chitosan only blocks *fat*, not calories from carbohydrates or protein. And also remember that there is a limit to how much Chitosan you can take, and how much fat you can block.) If you do not eat sensibly, the fat will overwhelm the Chitosan and it will do you little good. Indeed, the whole point of this approach is to cut down on your food consumption a little—an amount you can manage permanently—and let the Chitosan add its effect to your efforts. So, if you use the Fat Blocker Program as a guide for building lifelong eating and exercise habits—using the Chitosan to add to the effectiveness of your program—you will succeed.

Chitosan can help us accomplish a world of good. But, like most powerful substances, it must be used carefully and prudently. By following these rules, you can make Chitosan work *for* you, not against you.

+ Use Chitosan to help you get started. Start gradually. Don't try to do more than you know you can manage in the long run.

+ Follow the Fat Blocker Eating Program for good nutrition and good health.

+ Recognize that an occasional splurge will occur. But do not substitute splurge foods for the nutritious foods outlined in the Fat Blocker Eating Program, and keep your splurging as modest as you can (i.e., one piece of cake, not the whole cake).

+ Do not use Chitosan as an excuse to binge or engage in other unhealthy eating practices. If you do binge in spite of your best efforts, Chitosan can partially mitigate the effect of your transgression. But if you use Chitosan to permit yourself to binge, you will have allowed it to do you a lot of harm.

+ Do not take fat-soluble vitamins (vitamins A, D, or E) at the same time that you take Chitosan. (They may be less available for your body's use.)

+ Do not overuse Chitosan.

+ Do drink 8 glasses of water a day.

+ Remember: There is no substitute for nutritious eating and a regular exercise program. Chitosan can help you stay with your eating plan but it can't nourish your body, increase your physical fitness, or cause you to lose weight.

With Chitosan, you can *expect* to lose weight. Therefore, you will. Of course, some amount of determination and willpower is still required. But lack of willpower has not been your problem. Up to now, it was literally impossible for the large majority of overweight people to stick to their diets over the long haul. That was not because they lacked willpower or determination, but because the task couldn't be done. The history of literally tens of millions of overweight Americans proves the point. Anyone who has observed America's enormous achievements in almost every field of human endeavor knows that this is not a country made up of people who lack willpower!

But now, with Chitosan, losing weight and keeping it down is not only theoretically possible, it is a goal that you can achieve. And you should leave yourself with no doubt that you will.

10

---◆---

The Most Common Dieting Mistakes and How to Avoid Them

Most diets end in failure. We've all known people who have undergone dramatic weight losses only to pile the pounds back on, often with interest! Most of us have tried following stringent diets and then gone off them (with a vengeance!) because they were too difficult, too boring, or simply didn't work within our lifestyles. Obviously, with Chitosan, things will be different. That difference plays itself out by allowing people following my Fat Blocker Program to avoid the standard pitfalls of dieting.

What are they?

To answer that question, I've made a list of the 11 most common dieting pitfalls and I have shown you how Chitosan, together with my Fat Blocker Program, can help you avoid or minimize them.

1

Choosing a diet that is unbalanced in carbohydrates, protein, or fat

We've all heard about diets that require you to eat only proteins and fats, with little or no carbohydrates, causing your body to burn its own fat for energy. Other frequently recommended diets ask you to eat only 1 or 2 kinds of food repeatedly. Of course, you are likely to lose weight as long as you can manage to stay with these diets. But you won't be able to stay on them for very long. And a lot of the weight you lose will be water weight, quickly regained once you start eating normally again. (You can also lose a lot of essential minerals on these programs, leading to trouble.)

The Fat Blocker Program is a well-balanced program that offers all of the protein, carbohydrates, fat, vitamins, minerals, and phytochemicals that your body needs. And it's got plenty of variety. The beacon in the distance is a very healthy, low-fat, low-calorie, nutritionally perfect diet. But, like so many guiding lights, it is there to show the way, not for every one of us to attain. Rather, with Chitosan helping us as needed year after year, we can follow an entirely reasonable, sensible diet.

2

Choosing a diet plan that gives you tasteless food

People who are overweight enjoy eating. They enjoy good food. When they sit down to a meal, they want it to taste great. But too many diet plans call for a menu that would make an Indian fakir weep! No hearty eater will want to give up one of the great joys of his or her daily life.

The Fat Blocker Program is different. You don't have to give up decent, tasty food. Certainly, you will want to eat less of the fatty foods. And by correctly cooking and measuring, you will want to balance your food properly and cut down on fat you don't need. But you don't have to cut out all the fat you crave to make the food taste good. You don't have to stick to unadorned fish or chicken. You don't have to become a vegetarian unless · you wish to. Instead, you can eat sensibly, in reasonable quantities, enjoying your food—but losing weight because you are eating less while also exercising and, additionally, blocking part of the fat you consume with Chitosan.

3

Eating portions that are too large

Dieters commonly make small mistakes in judging portion sizes. But small errors like eating an extra ounce or two of meat, a large fruit (instead of a medium one) or an extra tablespoon of mayonnaise can slow or stop weight loss in its tracks. To avoid many of these small excesses as possible, I recommend the traditional techniques that work most of the time: Use a dieter's scale to weigh meat, fish, or poultry (weighing them cooked and boneless) and use measuring cups and spoons for other food groups. But, of course, we all know that these sensible approaches only go so far. Try as we may, small discrepancies will always tend to creep into our eating habits. Fortunately, that is where Chitosan steps in. It compensates for small, unintended amounts of excess fat. By combining care and Chitosan, we can avoid this all-too-common dieting error.

4

Adding extra fat while cooking

Just by forgetting to cut the extra fat off a cut of meat or leaving the skin on chicken, or by pouring a little extra oil in the frying pan, you can inadvertently add many grams of fat and therefore calories to a meal. So, if you use fat in cooking, always measure it carefully. And use a cooking spray, such as Pam, in preference to oil or butter when you fry. It adds only a tiny amount of fat, and the food cooks and tastes just the same. Also, considering sauteeing in water instead of oil. It doesn't work for everything. But a few drops of water is just as good (and, to my taste, even better) than the same amount of fat when you are sauteeing mushrooms or onions. Try experimenting; you'll be pleasantly surprised. The Fat Blocker Program encourages trimming excess fat from meats, discarding the skin, eating lean meats only, using low-fat or nonfat versions of margarine for cooking and nonfat salad dressing, milk (unless you hate it), and yogurt. Once again, if you decide to add fat to a meal because otherwise it's just not good enough to satisfy you, add as little as possible—and take Chitosan in advance to take care of the rest.

5

Following a diet plan that doesn't fit your lifestyle

You may find it a problem to follow a diet that say, calls for bacon, eggs, and grapefruit 3 times a day. How are you going to cook it at work? Are you going to make 2 separate dinners at home, one for you and one for the family? What about when you go out to eat?

The solution, as it is throughout this book, is to do the best you can, and use Chitosan to compensate for what you cannot manage. To repeat myself, the best you can is good enough.

Of course, there are some things you can do to help yourself. The first is that you should quickly enroll your whole family in the Fat Blocker Program. Since, unlike other diets you have been on, this one is not excessive in any respect, there is no reason why your spouse should not join in. All you are asking him or her to do is target the meals you eat to their best nutritional balance, and (if they feel they need to lose weight) eat a little less than before and, if necessary, take Chitosan. That's a long way from asking them to eat nothing but grapefruit or to adhere to a 1,200 calorie diet for the rest of their lives!

6

Following a diet that's too low in calories

It's virtually impossible for most people to follow a diet that provides too few calories for more than a short period of time.

Such deprivations hurt us literally and figuratively. In the course of our evolution, severe food shortages were commonplace. Therefore, we learned to grab for all the food we could get when the shortage was past. Those who didn't exhibit a sufficient level of gluttony didn't eat enough to survive the next famine—and their restraint genes died out with them. There is, therefore, nothing in our makeup to induce us to voluntarily quit eating. Of course, we can force ourselves to override our evolutionary pulls for a while. But, before long, we are bound to give in and grab for the food we want. Thus, we suffer the rebound effect that is almost inevitable after severely restrictive diets. We may go on a binge and eat everything in sight, or at the very least, become frustrated and depressed because we feel like failures.

To counteract the feeling of being too restrained in eating, my Fat Blocker Program never demands that you diet to the point of deprivation. Eat what you feel you must have, I insist, but try to cut down just a little. Let the Chitosan help you lose weight. As you lose it (and find yourself moving about more) your desire to eat will tend to slacken off and you will eat a little less.

Soon you will find yourself on a very positive upward spiral, with solid good health and an ideal weight profile being the beacon gleaming from not so terribly far away.

7

Exercising too little

Exercise is essential to weight loss, weight maintenance, and general good health. The Fat Blocker Program includes an excellent plan that makes it easy to start getting in shape: Take small steps! You'll find yourself increasing your exercise almost automatically. Eventually, chances are you'll reach or get close to ideal exercise levels—and then you'll stay there.

8

Failing to plan for special occasions

As I've often said, we live in the real world. Sometimes we can't (or don't want to) follow a strict diet. Birthday celebrations, anniversary parties, and holidays should be enjoyed. If we feel too deprived by our diets, we may just give up. By acknowledging your need for the occasional treat and using some extra Chitosan, you won't feel deprived; you won't feel guilty; and you will be able (and happy) to get back to your plan the next day (without having done it much harm in the meantime) and stick with it.

9

Focusing on weight, inches, or clothing size

Obsessing over a number on the scale, a dress size, or a waist measurement is bound to result in negative thinking, and at its extreme (which I see all too often in my patients), self-loathing. Don't let this happen to you. Ignore your weight and measurements for a while. Just start down your healthy eating–sensible exercise path, take Chitosan as appropriate, and smell the roses! Try it for as long as you can—say for a couple of months. Then see how you're doing. Don't expect miracles. But if you've lost even a few pounds or a half inch here or there, that is a sort of little miracle. Because, perhaps for the first time in your life, those pounds and inches are gone forever. As long as you stay on this simple, easy plan and take Chitosan, there can be no rebound effect.

10

Not allowing for personal vulnerability

Too many dieters take a hard-line approach with themselves. They *have* to be perfect; they *have* to follow their diets to the letter. If and when they fail to do so (as they must because their diet is too harsh to stay with), they beat themselves up, getting frustrated and eventually abandoning their diets. By starting out slowly, planning treats into your diet, asking yourself only for small improvements in your food intake and exercise patterns at the outset, but blocking many of the fat calories with Chitosan, this program provides the best of both worlds—a chance to be less than perfect, and the assurance that you are not ruining your health or waistline!

11

Forgetting to reward oneself

Following even a sensible, "easy" food plan can sometimes be tough. The Fat Blocker Program permits rewards in the form of "splurges," but it also recommends that we reward ourselves in non-food ways. Take a walk, buy yourself something new to wear, arrange a romantic getaway to a fancy hotel. Above all, treat yourself well. Patting yourself on the back, telling yourself you've done a good job and doing something just for the fun of it are all integral parts of a successful weight-loss program. Reward yourself; you deserve it.

You Can Do It!

When you embark on your healthy-living, weight-loss program, this time things will be different. Perhaps for the first time in your life, you will be starting on a program that will last you for the rest of it. This is because the Fat Blocker Program has it all—a healthful, easy-to-follow, nutritious eating program, an excellent, invigorating but easy exercise program, a positive attitude, and the extra help you need from Chitosan.

So, go for it. With these four vital tools, you *can* conquer your weight problem and give your body the irreplaceable gift of superb health.

11

$\blacklozenge$

Dieters Beware

Back in 1969, an overweight man named Frank came to my office to see me, demanding that I give him those special shots.

"What shots?" I asked.

"The diet shots," Frank replied. "The ones that make you lose weight. You gave them to my friend and they were great! I want to lose 50 pounds in 2 months because if I don't I'll lose my job as an airline pilot. And then I'll also be healthier, because I'll be thinner."

I told Frank that I hadn't given anyone diet shots and didn't know what he was referring to, but this tall, obese man was insistent. "I want those special shots. I have to lose weight." After careful questioning, I discovered that he was talking about HCG shots, the diet rage of the day. HCG stands for horse chorionic gonadotrophin, a substance made from the urine of pregnant mares.

I understood why he was so desperate to slim down, so I acceded to his demands for the special shots. I gave him instructions on low-fat eating and told him to come to my office every morning for a shot.

So every morning Frank came in and my nurse gave him a special shot that consisted of $1/2$ cc of water. She also weighed him, and acting on my instructions, scolded him. It didn't matter what he weighed, how much he had gained or lost, she scolded him and told him to eat more vegetables and whole grains and less fatty corned beef, ice cream, and candy.

You know what? My special shot diet worked! Frank lost weight. Obviously it wasn't because of the injections, but because Frank believed that they would help. His belief gave him the motivation to stick with the simple dietary instructions I gave him (and the admonishments of my nurse), and he lost weight. As I recall, he lost 50 pounds in 12 weeks and was able to keep his job. Unfortunately, when the special shots were discontinued he gained it all back.

Frank's story illustrates the final three points of the Fat Blocker Program. He had unreasonable expectations, he confused being very thin with being healthy, and he was desperate to try the latest weight-loss fad.

Like so many of us, Frank had unrealistic goals. He wanted to look like a dashing, handsome, slim, young, leading-man type, even though his natural build was on the round side, making him closer to the chubby, best-friend type. Frank would have to starve himself in order to get down to a weight that made him look anything like a leading man. And even then he wouldn't succeed, because he would become gaunt and emaciated, not handsome and fit. Of course, I understood Frank's desire. As a teenager and young man I wanted huge muscles, but could never seem to develop them, no matter how hard I tried. I finally had to accept the fact that I was just not the body-builder type, and was better off developing an appreciation for the mind and body that nature had granted me.

Frank also believed that if he were thin he would automatically be healthy. Would that it were so! As pointed out earlier, low poundage does not necessarily equal good health. Achieving ideal body weight is desirable since there is a positive correlation between health and slimness, but rapidly losing lots of weight or keeping your weight unnaturally low by eating a nutritionally unbalanced diet can work *against* your health rather than *for* it. Certainly, keeping your weight low by using highly potent prescription drugs is a terrible thing to do to yourself.

And finally, Frank was willing to try any fad weight-loss program or diet that came along as long as it took off the pounds. What he didn't know was this: Practically every single diet he'd ever heard about *would* work—but only for a little while. They'll all knock the pounds off (and some will do so quickly) but they all also suffer from one big flaw—like my special shot diet, they're temporary fixes. You lose the weight, then you put it right back on. And many times, you put more back on than you lost in the first place. The only way I have ever heard of to safely, permanently, and reliably lose weight while building better health is to use my Fat Blocker Program (in context with the lifelong, sensible, doable eating and exercise program outlined in this book). It will work for almost everyone; fad diets will work for almost no one.

To prove my point, let's take a closer look at some of these popular fad diets, as well as certain weight-loss products and surgeries to see why they *all* fail in the long run—and why some of them are downright dangerous.

Fad Diets, from Atkins to the Zone

I've selected these diets for discussion because millions of dieters are using them right at this very moment. You can find many of the books that promote these diets on the shelves of your local bookstore, either in their original forms or in a slightly altered version.

DR. ATKINS' DIET REVOLUTION[1]

A phenomenally popular diet that swept the nation in the 1970s, the Atkins Diet is still being used today. That's a shame, for in my opinion it is nutritionally unsound and potentially dangerous. Atkins claims that most overweight people suffer from metabolic imbalances cause by a carbohydrate intolerance.

His solution is to eliminate carbohydrates altogether during the diet, then keep them cut way down permanently. Promising that you will not be hungry, Atkins encourages you to cut back on carbohydrates, not calories. You can eat to your heart's content, he asserts, because when you eliminate carbohydrates from the diet, your desire for food is diminished.

Atkins and others who promote high-protein diets are simply trotting out an old idea devised by a Victorian-era doctor. According to the high-protein proponents, the high protein/low carbohydrate diet is supposed to force the body to rid itself of stored fats faster than usual. What really happens is that the poorly metabolized fatty acids (called ketones) that result from this diet cause you to urinate greater amounts of body water, along with magnesium, potassium, and other important minerals. It may *seem* like you're losing weight, but that weight is quickly replaced when you take a drink. It's all smoke and mirrors—you think you're losing a lot of weight but you're really not. And meanwhile, all those ketones in your bloodstream can harm your health.

Another dangerous aspect of the high-protein diets is bone loss (osteoporosis). Thinning of the bones, commonly caused by loss of calcium, is a common problem for seniors, especially elderly women. Thinned bones are more likely to fracture under pressure. Even a very slight touch is all it takes to crack the bones of some osteoporosis victims. High-protein diets cause us to lose dangerously high amounts of calcium in the urine. Not only that, but the excess sulfur and nitrogen from the proteins can literally leach calcium right out of bones.

The diet promises that you can eat luxuriously—heavy cream, butter, mayonnaise, cheeses, meats, fish, fowl. A small amount of these foods can add flavor to the diet, as well as certain nutrients, but to base a diet on these high-protein, high-fat foods is folly. Even Dr. Atkins admits that his program is unbalanced. This diet revolution is, in the author's own words, "deliberately unbalanced . . . to counteract the metabolic imbalances that cause people to get fat in the first place." He's right about the first part, the diet is unbalanced and filled with potentially dangerous amounts of fat. Eliminating carbohydrates from the diet and replacing them with protein and fat can only encourage heart disease, cancer, and a host of other ailments. As for the second part about metabolic imbalances causing obesity, well, relatively few of us are overweight because of metabolic imbalances. I tell my patients to read the Atkins and other high-protein diet books, if they want, then do the exact opposite. The best approach is to eat plenty of complex carbohydrates (found especially in fresh vegetables and whole grains) and *reduce* your fat intake by sensible eating coupled with Chitosan. That's the basis for healthy weight loss and healthy living.

BODYFUELING[2]

This "groundbreaking" approach promises that you'll be able to eat plenty of delicious foods and keep your metabolism humming by having you discard the poor fueling that has been harming you. But first comes the inspirational step of learning to think of food as fuel, not the enemy. Developing the proper mindset and proper goals will help you fuel your future rather than concentrating on dieting to lose weight. Although author Robyn Landis recommends a low-fat diet, she also insists that calories don't count, so you can eat as much as you like as long as you exercise and use the right kind of mental and dietary fuel. This confusing, unfounded program is best left on the shelf.

DR. ABRAVANEL'S BODY TYPE DIET

I've known Elliot Abravanel for some time, and while I enjoy his company, I disagree with the premise of his diet. Although his program is no longer well known, the underlying theory resurfaces every so often in a new guise. The basic idea is that we all have different body types and each type requires a different diet. In Dr. Abravanel's version, there are four types of bodies: the thyroid type, the adrenal type, the pituitary type, and (for women only) the gonadal type. Depending on body type, an individual needs to eat a certain way or he or she will suffer.

Dieters take a lengthy bodytype personal metabolic inventory to discover their type, then go on a 1,200-calorie-a-day diet appropriate for their type for 3 weeks. During the fourth week they consume a purification diet, then begin the cycle all over again. This continues until the weight has dropped to the desired level. The basic food plans of this diet, which are based on fresh vegetables and fruits, whole grains, fish, and poultry, can be quite healthful. But the underlying rationale (body type) has not stood the test of time.

THE NEW CABBAGE SOUP DIET[3]

This diet qualifies for entry into the Single Food Diet Sweepstakes, and states right up front that you should only stay on it for 7 days with the goal of experiencing the gratification of quick weight loss. Then the author suggests that you go off the diet for 2 weeks before trying it for another 7 days. Why the on-off approach? Because, in the author's own words, "The New Cabbage Soup Diet is not appropriate for long-term use. It is not intended as a substitute for good long-term eating habits. The diet may be used for up to a week, but after a week the reader should switch to a *normal nutritionally balanced diet* [italics mine] . . . The reader should not use the New Cabbage Soup Diet too frequently even with 2-week or longer intervals in between uses." When the diet's own author admits this right up front, you know that there are serious problems with the diet. If nothing else, it's meant to be a quick fix that teaches you nothing about proper lifelong eating habits. So even though cabbage is one of my favorite foods (I eat a bowlful a week), I suggest you avoid this diet.

Cabbage soup diets have appeared under various names, including the Fat Burning Soup Diet, the New Mayo Clinic Diet, and the Scared Heart Hospital Diet. Just to set the record straight, there's nothing especially fat-burning about eating cabbage soup, and this diet is *not* associated with the Mayo Clinic or any of the many hospitals that go by the name of Sacred Heart.

THE CARBOHYDRATE CRAVER'S DIET

Like the Body Type Diet, the Carbohydrate Craver's Diet seems to be continually in circulation, and revised versions with new names and slightly different rules regularly surface. Plenty of carbohydrates are allocated for each meal, and often carbohydrate-laden snacks are encouraged between meals. Why so many carbohydrates? Because, say the authors of these diets, the human brain craves carbos. If we don't eat enough carbohydrates we'll be driven to overeat, so it's best to satisfy the natural cravings and quell the wild desire to eat other foods. You can lose weight on some versions of this diet, because they're typically low calorie. But depending on the version, you may wind up with a nutritionally unbalanced regimen that has refined carbohydrates sending your blood sugar up and down like a roller coaster. Moreover, as with all other low-calorie diets, most people cannot stick to them—so, naturally, they don't work. However, if you combine a nutritionally balanced, moderate-calorie diet with Chitosan, you will be able to lower your fat intake (and with it your calorie consumption) by enough to lose weight and keep it off.

THE DOCTOR'S QUICK WEIGHT LOSS DIET

Also known as the Stillman Diet for its creator, Dr. Irwin Stillman, this diet is based on the idea that the body deals one way with protein, and another way with fats and carbohydrates. According to the theories underlying the diet, the body expends more energy digesting a protein molecule than it does digesting fat or carbohydrate molecules. Thus, eating a high-protein diet will cause the body to burn up lots more calories than eating a high-carbohydrate or high-fat diet. The increased SDA (specific dynamic action) caused by burning protein supposedly prompts the body to burn an extra 275 calories a day.

Water also plays a major role in the Quick Weight Loss Diet. Eight glasses of water per day, plus additional quantities of coffee, tea, and diet soda are prescribed in order to wash the ketones (the residue created by incomplete fat burning) out of the body. Because of this, many people call this plan the Water Diet.

You can lose weight on the Stillman Diet. You can also harm your health, for the protein and fat-heavy regimen is nutritionally unbalanced and very bad for your heart. As with most fad diets, once you go off the diet you will, undoubtedly, regain the weight you lost. I've treated many patients who have plugged up their arteries with fat and cholesterol from this type of diet. Remember: The high protein you get from these diets is accompanied by high fat—a potentially lethal combination. However, in one respect I agree with Dr. Stillman: You should drink 8 glasses of water a day.

EAT RIGHT FOR YOUR TYPE[4]

According to the authors of this book and eating plan, your blood type determines what you should be eating and how you should exercise, among other things. For example, people with Type O blood should consume a high-protein, low-carbohydrate diet, cutting out wheat and most other grains, while exercising vigorously. Those with Type A blood, however, do better as vegetarians, and should adopt golf, yoga, or other gentle exercises. Having Type B blood means that you should consume a varied diet, including the dairy products that seem to trouble Type O and Type A. Moderate exercise such as swimming or walking is best for the Bs. If you have Type AB blood you have the combined pluses and minuses of A and B types, and should use relaxation techniques and calming exercises.

This is another program that is based on only the weakest of evidence. Following a certain diet simply because you have one type of blood or another, without regard for the diet's effects or its risk of promoting heart disease, cancer, or other diseases, makes no sense. As a physician I can tell you that this approach is not for you, regardless of your blood type.

FIT FOR LIFE[5]

This 1985 diet was wildly popular for years, and the book that describes the diet still sells well. The program, devised by

Harvey and Marilyn Diamond, is based on the principles of Natural Hygiene, including the theory that the "body is always striving for health and that it achieves this by continuously cleansing itself of deleterious waste material."[6] They say the body has specific cycles during the day: From noon to 8 P.M. the body is appropriating (digesting the food you've eaten), from 8 P.M. until 4 A.M. the body is assimilating (absorbing and using nutrients), and from 4 A.M. to noon it is eliminating debris from the food and bodily wastes. According to the Diamonds, we should synchronize our eating to these cycles, eating the appropriate amounts of certain types of foods at each meal. This will ensure that our bodies will rid themselves of dangerous wastes and remain slim.

The Diamonds encourage dieters to combine foods in specific ways that will make sure that nothing is left to "rot" in the stomach. They preach the importance of having no more than one concentrated food in the stomach at a time, eating only A.M. foods in the morning and P.M. foods later in the day, and many other unusual rules. With their plan, what you wind up eating is not a bad diet, but the theories behind this regimen were questioned long ago. Rather than adhering to a so-so diet based on incorrect principles, you're much better off blocking fat with Chitosan and a scientifically based, patient-tested, safe, and effective healthy eating regimen.

THE NEW HILTON HEAD METABOLISM DIET[7]

"It's not your fault if you're overweight," says the author of this diet. Obesity is supposedly caused by faulty metabolism, so you should think of your weight problem as a chronic disease that must be cured. The Hilton Head Diet promises to increase your metabolic rate so that you'll burn more calories—without added effort. It's also supposed to change your body chemistry to make managing your weight easier. All this, while encouraging you to eat *more* meals than before. Sounds great doesn't it? But wait!

The diet's first key ingredient is a low-fat, high-complex carbohydrate eating regimen, which is good. But that's as far as I can agree with the Hilton Head Diet. I see no basis for their claim that the body chemistry is somehow changed, so that you can eat more and lose weight without effort. I also take issue with their idea of "dietary stairstepping." The author suggests that you divide your desired weight loss into small steps to be tackled one at a time, with time off for rejuvenating your metabolism in between. While it can be a good idea to move forward very gradually, setting your goals at manageable levels so that you can achieve them and stay with them, this "stairstepping" approach seems to admit that you cannot stay with the diet. Why else would you have to take time off to rejuvenate? That hardly suggests that you will be able to stay with this approach indefinitely.

IMMUNE POWER DIET

Presented by Stuart Berger, M.D., the author of *The Southampton Diet*, this diet is based on the unproved premise that fat cells cause a terrible "tug of war" between you and your own immune system. As your immune system weakens, so the theory goes, you are more likely to become fat. Although Dr. Berger was correct in asserting that excess fat is bad for the immune system, his 1,200-calorie-a-day program is unbalanced and far too rigorous, and his theory that a weak immune system makes you fat is unfounded.

THE "IT'S NOT YOUR FAULT YOU'RE FAT" DIET

This is another version of the allergy diets that pop up regularly. Its author, Marshall Mandell, M.D., says that we may be simultaneously allergic and addicted to certain foods. Eating those foods makes us ill and overweight, but we can't help eating them. The doctor's solution to this allergy/addiction is the Rotary Diet, which dates back to 1934. The diet employs a 21-day rotation of 10 foods per day, with no single food eaten more than once every 4 days. Although the premise is enticing, it simply does not stand up to scientific scrutiny. Many people are allergic to various foods, but there is no evidence that this diet will help them or you become healthier and slimmer for life. The basic premise of the diet is unsound. While it may have some value for dealing with food allergies, I do not believe it has value as a weight-loss diet.

LIQUID PROTEIN DIETS

The diets, which were all the rage in the 1970s contained large amounts of protein but very few carbohydrates. You can lose weight on liquid-protein diets, and/or other high-protein, low-carbohydrate diets. But you can also lose your health, and possibly your life. Here's how these diets work: Your body can burn either carbohydrates, fat, or protein for energy. Your body prefers to burn carbohydrates because they are burned the most efficiently and are the safest energy source. Carbohydrates are stored as an energy source in the liver and muscles in the form of glycogen. But after a couple of days on a high-protein, low-carbohydrate diet, the glycogen will be completely depleted. As they are exhausted, your body begins to lose a great deal of water, causing you to lose a lot of weight. You also lose a great deal of sodium and other minerals, especially magnesium and potassium (which are essential for the health of your heart). As you continue on the diet your body goes into an unnatural state (ketosis) due to the influx of ketones (incompletely burned fat) into the bloodstream. This causes the blood to become more acidic and is dangerous to your health. (This is especially dangerous when you're pregnant, since ketones in the bloodstream can harm the fetus. Don't *ever* go on this kind of diet if you are or might possibly be pregnant.) As water and precious minerals are lost, and the level of ketones in your bloodstream rises, your immune system may become damaged.

Meanwhile, your body will be searching for a different energy source since there are no carbohydrates left in the body. Seizing upon any fat or protein it can find, it begins to break down organs and muscles to release protein for energy. This is akin to pulling down the walls in your house to burn in the fireplace for warmth. It may be effective for a while, but disastrous in the long run.

If, and only if, you are perfectly healthy, you may be able to get away with this kind of diet for a while; but even if you are in perfect health, you will be taking years off your life. You may weather the storm now, but the damage you sustain will take its toll at some point later in your life.

Liquid-protein diets attempted to get around some of these problems by supplying the dieter with predigested animal protein. It was believed that the body would burn the liquid protein for energy when its supply of carbohydrates was gone, rather than eating into the muscles and organs. Unfortunately, the theory doesn't pan out. What really happens is that many people suffer marked fatigue, dehydration, cardiac arrhythmias, and other serious problems. In the 1970s when these kinds of diets were the rage, they caused the deaths of over 50 people.

THE MCDOUGALL PROGRAM FOR MAXIMUM WEIGHT LOSS[8]

Dr. John McDougall is a very likable man. I've been a guest on his radio program and I admire his desire to prevent disease. At the age of 18 he suffered a stroke that left him partially paralyzed on his left side, and at 25 he underwent exploratory surgery for severe abdominal problems. He developed his McDougall Program to help himself heal, and later prescribed it to his patients. I like the basis of his plan, which emphasizes vegetables, fruits, and complex carbohydrates. For most people who simply want to lose weight, however, his otherwise sound program is too difficult to follow because it's too restrictive. However, without the excessive restriction and with the addition of Chitosan, this program is really sound. It happens to be what the Fat Blocker Program is all about!

THE ROTATION DIET[9]

A 1986 entry into the world of fad diets, the Rotation Diet argues, correctly, that diets with severe calorie limitations fail because of the innate starvation response. When we restrict our intake, according to this diet's author, our bodies respond by slowing everything down (dropping the basal metabolic rate). A low-calorie diet will knock off pounds, but it will also slow the metabolism, and it will take less food than ever to make us fat again.

The diet's author suggests that the only way to avoid this starvation response is to rotate through a dietary cycle, with each cycle supplying a different amount of calories. Thus, a woman on the Rotation Diet would consume 600 calories a day for the first 3 days, 900 per day for the next 4 days, then 1,200 per day for a week. A man would eat 1,200 per day for the first 3 days, 1,500 per day for 4 days, and 1,800 per day for a week. The entire cycle is repeated once, then the dieter stops dieting completely for a week, a month, or as long as he or she feels is proper. After this vacation from dieting, the dieter repeats the entire process (2 cycles and stop) until the desired weight is reached.

This 3-stage, twice-repeated, on-and-off is supposed to prevent the starvation response while motivating you to succeed. You will allegedly look forward to every new dietary cycle with eager anticipation. Like most fad diets, this one is based on science of suspicious origins. The on-and-off cycles sound like they will encourage bingeing or other poor eating habits as the dieter hurries to eat whatever she likes before going on the diet again. What does the dieter learn about lifelong healthful eating habits from a plan such as this? Nothing much. You're much better off adopting a consistent eating plan that fits comfortably into your life and sticking with it.

THE COMPLETE SCARSDALE MEDICAL DIET

This popular high-protein diet swept the country many years ago. Authored by Herman Tarnower, M.D., it was featured in the *New York Times, Family Circle,* and many other newspapers and magazines. The Scarsdale Diet encourages you to eat lots of meat and claims that you can lose up to a pound a day. The foods that may be eaten every day are carefully controlled, but portion sizes are pretty much up to the dieter. They are only warned that they should not eat so much that their stomachs become uncomfortably overloaded. I don't believe that this will work with people who tend to overeat as a rule. Simply telling them not to stuff themselves until they can't eat anymore is not exactly the cornerstone of a healthful, lifelong eating regimen. It might work for people who are already used to moderate portions, but many obese people are accustomed to eating quite a bit.

And not only are the parameters weak and poorly defined, the Scarsdale Diet is potentially dangerous. Like the Atkins Diet and many others, it works on the principle of inducing an unnatural state—ketosis—into the body. Even Dr. Tarnower, who devised the diet, warns you not to stay on it for more than 2 weeks at a time because of the dangers of ketosis, which can include lethargy, weakness, coma, and even death. Dieters who follow this program may also become deficient in vitamin A, vitamin D, and calcium, while simultaneously overdosing on protein. We've been taught to believe that protein is good, and the more we eat the better. But the truth is that excess protein can lead to an increased risk of osteoporosis and kidney stones, while the high fat associated with high protein increases the risk of cardiovascular disease.

THE *SCENT*SATIONAL WEIGHT LOSS DIET[10]

Dr. Alan Hirsch, author of this diet, argues that we suffer from an overabundance of food, a condition that's become common only during the last century or so. We must fight our evolutionary tendency to gain and store weight during the winter and times of plenty, just in case the food runs out and we're faced with famine. Indeed, the evolutionary chain was able to produce us only because our ancestors were good at storing fat that could be used when the food ran out. But changing our inborn patterns is difficult to do in the modern world when we have consistent access to so much food. So far, so good. He is right that this is the genesis of our problem.

The solution to this problem can be found right in our own noses, according to Hirsch. Simply sniffing certain odors is often all it takes to satisfy hunger cravings. Hirsch recommends that we carry little tubes that contain the scents of bananas, apples, or other foods, and that we sniff them throughout the day. Each time you sniff, he says, inhale 3 times in each nostril. Hirsch suggests that you use different scents during the day so that you don't tire of the same one. If you like, you can work the program with a smell buddy.

You don't have to carry the tubes if you'd rather not. You can simply smell your food before you eat it to start stimulating the satiety center in your brain as soon as possible. If you do rely on sniffing your food, rather than using the tubes, you are supposed to eat hot foods whenever possible, for they release more odor than cold dishes. Eat fresh foods, and pour on those herbs and spices. It also helps to blow bubbles with your food in order to release the scent of the food into the air, which you then inhale.

Hirsch feels that sniffing to stimulate the satiety center is all it takes to trigger less eating and weight loss. "You won't be given a list of foods you must eat at breakfast or lunch," he says. "You will not be weighing your foods or counting calories."

Sniffing away the pounds is an enticing idea but I'd like to see some more scientific studies to back this theory up. Even if it really does work, which seems intuitively unlikely, this diet is not a good idea because it teaches nothing about how to balance your diet correctly or achieve anything approaching a lifelong path for good health.

WHY DO I EAT WHEN I'M NOT HUNGRY?[11]

The key to this program is applied kinesiology, which the author describes as dealing with the way in which "the body's electrical energy . . . affects the well-being of the physical body." Ailments are treated by correcting disturbances in the flow. The diet's author, psychologist Roger Callahan, is primarily interested in treating food addiction, which he feels prevents countless dieters from losing weight and keeping it off. He argues that food addiction is caused by anxiety, which is in turn due to imbalances in the body's electrical-energetic system. In other words, we don't overeat or eat the wrong foods because we're really hungry. Rather we chow down because the food tranquilizes us and reduces our anxiety.

Dr. Callahan proposes to solve this complex psychological problem by having us tap certain parts of the body in order to rebalance its electrical-energetic system, reduce or eliminate anxiety, and eliminate food addiction. Specific eye movements, stretching, humming, and counting are also part of the Callahan Techniques.

The book promises that you will lose weight because the Callahan Techniques work 95 percent of the time, in just minutes. There are separate treatments for reducing the urge to eat, gluttony, impatience, as well as a "Treatment For The Prevention Of Addiction" and "The Thirty-Day Food Addiction Program" for those already hooked.

Tapping, moving your eyes back and forth, stretching, humming, and counting will undoubtedly help some people by focusing their attention on something other than food. But this program has no scientific basis to support it and is based entirely on the author's experiences with patients. Dr. Callahan is certainly well meaning and eager to help people. I'm sure that his good feelings about these techniques transfer to his patients, creating a temporary placebolike effect. That's well and good, but it's also temporary, and the patients learn nothing about exchanging old, unhealthy habits for new and better ones.

THE ZONE[12]

Barry Sears' best-selling diet asserts that carbohydrates are the primary villain in the battle against fat and disease. "All conventional weight reduction diets are hormonally incorrect," he says, insisting that the key to achieving great physical, mental, and emotional health is learning "how to control hormonal responses to food." That's your passport into what he calls the zone. To get into the zone, Dr. Sears tells you to eat a Zone-favorable diet from which you receive 30 percent of your calories from fat, 30 percent from protein, and 40 percent from carbohydrates. Unfortunately, bread, pasta, rice, and other grains are restricted, which robs the dieter of many nutrients and health-enhancing properties. This diet is actually a step *backward* toward the standard high-fat, high-protein diet that propelled so many millions of Americans to early encounters with heart disease, cancer, and sometimes death.

Weight-Loss Products

STIMULANTS

These diet pills, which are actually brain stimulants, are so popular that variations of them are sold in supermarkets under brand names such as Dexatrim. One common amphetamine-like drug, a central nervous stimulant called benzedrine, was first used as a nasal inhalant to ease breathing. It was discontinued, however, when it was found that people were taking it out of the inhalant and using it for the wrong reasons.

Benzedrine, dexedrine, and other amphetamines, commonly known as speed, work by cutting the appetite. But when you stop taking them your appetite returns, often with a vengeance, resulting in a greater weight gain than the original loss. Amphetamines also have potentially serious side effects, including heart palpitations, elevated blood pressure, sleep disturbances, trembling, nervousness, anxiety, agitation, and panic attacks. They may even precipitate heart attacks.

And the risks are not confined to prescription-only drugs. Many over-the-counter weight-loss pills at your pharmacy contain a substance called phenylpropanolamine as their main ingredient. Over the years, I have seen numerous patients develop high blood pressure and heart arrhythmias after exposure to this substance.

Taking these drugs (prescription or over-the-counter) is of no value for long-term, healthful weight loss, and may also lead to dependency. Kitty Dukakis, wife of 1988 presidential candidate Michael Dukakis, created quite a stir when she admitted to having been hooked on amphetamines for over 20 years. I have even seen children stoned and ill from weight-loss pills (which they take for the high). Do yourself a favor and don't get started on any of them.

HORMONES

Most hormones, including estrogen, progesterone, and testosterone, do not help you lose weight. Instead, they can actually cause you to *gain* weight. Human growth hormone (HGH) will reduce body fat and increase lean body muscle, but will not reduce overall body weight. These hormones have special uses and shouldn't be utilized for weight loss.

"JIGGLE" MACHINES

Back in the 1960s, the older 4 of my 7 children used to love to go with me to the Los Angeles Athletic Club. There, in the weight room, were several of what my kids called the "jiggle" machines. They'd wrap the wide belts around their waists, lean back, hit the switch, and jiggle away. My son Barry especially liked to sing while in the machine because all the shaking filled his voice with vibrato. These machines are fun, and may even be relaxing to some people, but they didn't help anyone to lose weight. Unfortunately, you can't jiggle away the pounds. You have to decrease your caloric intake and step up your energy expenditure to do that.

PHEN-FEN

This "hot" weight-loss gimmick is ballyhooed in newspaper advertisements everywhere and is spread far and wide across the Internet. Phen-Fen is short for phentermine and fenfluramine, 2 drugs that influence the neurotransmitters (messengers) in the brain.

Phentermine alters blood flow, heartbeat, and other body functions by making more dopamine and norepinephrine available to brain cells, which reduces appetite. Fenfluramine increases the amount of a neurotransmitter called serotonin, which plays a role in regulating appetite and mood, so appetite is further reduced. The 2 drugs, which showed limited promise in treating obesity when used separately, did much better when combined.

Like all drugs, these 2 can have side effects, including dry mouth, jitteriness, drowsiness, diarrhea, nausea, headaches, high blood pressure, insomnia, and sexual dysfunction. There's also the risk of pulmonary hypertension and heart failure, as well as the potential for subtle brain damage. If you use these two drugs, you must be monitored carefully by a knowledgeable, nutritionally minded physician, and you should not take them for longer than 3 months.

Redux (dexfenfluramine) is the newest weight-loss drug. Its use must be monitored by a knowledgeable physician, for it has appreciable side effects similar to those seen with Phen-Fen. It must not be used for more than 3 months, and should be accompanied by nutritional and behavioral training.

PROMISES, PROMISES

Every once in a while a new diet plan surfaces, promising that you will lose all the weight you desire if you simply make a promise to yourself that sounds something like this: "Self, if you don't lose X pounds in Y days, you'll have to do Z." The thing you have to do (Z) is very unpleasant. In the Blackmail Diet,[13] author John Bear promised himself that if he didn't lose 75 pounds in one year, he would donate $5,000 to the Nazis. The authors of the Blackmail Diet and similar plans assert that with powerful motivation you can't help but toe the line and drop the pounds.

If the threat of having to do something repugnant helps to

motivate you, fine. I find that motivation works much more effectively when it's positive, rather than negative. Eating healthfully shouldn't be something that we do only when the threat of something horrible hangs over our heads. It should be something we do naturally and enjoy. But even if negative motivation works fine for you, it still must be coupled with a safe, effective, lifelong program of proper eating and exercise. And that must involve goals you can live with easily. Perhaps you can manage, by placing yourself under a sufficient threat, to stick to a super-aggressive diet for a while—even a year. But once the threat is lifted, you'll assuredly start eating again, and probably more than ever. Cutting back by eating somewhat less and using Chitosan works; trying to cut back massively just won't work.

SAUNAS AND STEAM BATHS

I love to sit in the sauna or steam room at my gym, although 5 minutes is about all I can handle. All that heat and moisture certainly feel great after a workout. But don't fool yourself into thinking that they're effective weight-loss tools. Yes, you may sweat out some water, but any weight loss that occurs is very temporary. In fact, if you lose more than a tiny bit of weight in a sauna, you're risking severe loss of body fluid and dehydration.

I don't recommend a sauna or steam bath if you have high blood pressure. The heat is vasodilating, which means that it causes blood vessels to open up. This can alter your circulation and lower your blood pressure, which in turn can cause transient ischemic heart attacks and strokes in certain people.

STARCH BLOCKERS

Products that interfere with the body's ability to absorb starch were especially popular in the late 1970s and early 1980s. In 1982 alone, you could choose from among some 100 different starch blockers, and over 1 million starch-blocking pills were popped daily.

The theory behind the starch blocker is simple: If you absorb fewer carbohydrates (starches), you'll lose weight. But in real life the theory just doesn't pan out.[14] Besides, carbohydrates should make up about 70 percent of our daily diets. It's the *fat* we want to reduce, not the carbohydrates. By all means use Chitosan, the Fat Blocker. Block the right thing!

WATER PILLS

Water pills, which we doctors call diuretics, have long been a popular weight-loss aid. The idea is that if we're overweight because we tend to retain excess water, then all we have to do is take a few diuretics (water pills) to flush it all out, and we'll be slim and trim. But no one becomes obese because he or she retains water. In fact, the percentage of body weight that can be attributed to water actually *drops* when one becomes obese. Sure, water pills will cause a slight weight loss due to the elimination of water. But those pounds will quickly be regained. So, when all is said and done, taking water pills is pointless and greatly increases the risk of dehydration.

If water retention is really a problem for you, it may be a sign of a medical problem such as an underactive thyroid gland, an overactive adrenal gland, congestive heart failure, kidney failure, or some other serious condition. See your doctor.

All in all, water pills are not safe, sane diet aids. Their effect is very temporary, and overindulgence may lead to dehydration. To make matters worse, using these water pills can cause you to lose magnesium and potassium, two minerals essential for a healthy cardiovascular system.

Weight Loss Surgeries

LIPOSUCTION

This surgical technique involves vacuuming the fat out of the hips, abdomen, or other areas and has some value in dealing with stubborn, localized fat. Responsible surgeons often ask me to help their patients reduce their general body fat down to healthy, slim levels before their localized fat is sucked out. This is a surgical procedure that, like all surgeries, carries definite risks, including infections and, very rarely, even death. One patient I know suffered severe peritonitis after a very good plastic surgeon removed her abdominal fat. A full year passed before the poor woman completely recovered. Even if your liposuction procedure goes perfectly, it's not necessarily the end of your problem, because the fat cells that remain can grow to tremendous size if your poor eating and lifestyle habits continue. In any case, this procedure has little to do with your actual health. It's merely cosmetic. You may look better, but you won't feel much different.

STOMACH STAPLING AND THE INTESTINAL BYPASS

These drastic remedies require full-blown surgery. For stomach stapling, a portion of the stomach is stapled shut, reducing the size of the portion of the stomach that receives the food. The theory behind stapling is that if you can't hold as much food as you used to, you'll eat less and lose weight. The intestinal bypass surgery takes a different approach, disconnecting or removing a portion of the small intestines (where much of the food we eat is actually absorbed into the body). The idea is that food that can't be absorbed in the shortened small intestine will simply pass out of the body.

Both of these surgeries have an enticing premise: Don't worry about what you eat, it can't harm you once we doctors have surgically altered your body. Unfortunately, the surgeries themselves can be dangerous. Any time you undergo any surgery you run the risk of suffering complications—including death. In addition, stomach stapling can cause scarring, eating can become uncomfortable, and overeating can cause the stomach to stretch out or pop its staples so that it returns to its original size, making the entire procedure a waste of time. Complications of the intestinal bypass include tremendous diarrhea, urinary stones, infections, liver failure, and malnutrition. (Being unable to absorb excess calories may be great, but the surgery also cuts down on your ability to absorb nutrients.)

Stomach stapling and intestinal bypasses take very paternalistic approaches to weight loss (i.e., "Don't worry about anything; we'll take care of you."). The people who subject themselves to these surgeries don't learn how to eat or exercise or otherwise improve their health. In fact, they knowingly risk their health. Such drastic surgeries may be necessary for the morbidly obese who are in danger of dying from complications of the weight. While there are successes, I have treated many patients who've had such horrendous side effects from these surgeries that they've sworn "never again." With a very few exceptions, it's much better to avoid stapling and intestinal bypass altogether.

There's Only One Way

Fad diets, pills, "metabolic enhancers," devices, shots, and surgeries will come and go. But there's only one way to lose weight and keep it off—eat sensibly, exercise, use Chitosan, and live for optimal health. If you focus on great health in this way (with just a little attention to your waistline), you'll lose weight while setting the stage for a long, zestful, healthy life.

12

◆

The Weight Is Over

I've written quite a few words, explained many principles, and reviewed scientific studies. Now there's only more thing to say. Actually, I've already said it but I'll repeat myself, for it is the single most important part of this or any other program: You *can* do it! As Ralph Waldo Emerson noted, we are what we think all day long. If we think of ourselves as being slim and healthy, easily able to follow the Fat Blocker Program, then we are well on our way toward accomplishing our goals.

But, of course, Emerson didn't mean that we could accomplish the impossible. To fly, you need an airplane. Believing otherwise is delusional madness. And to lose weight and keep it off permanently, the equivalent of the airplane is Chitosan. With the means to succeed *and* the belief in ourselves, success is all but assured.

The first step in losing weight and living healthfully is to master the principles of blocking fat and to establish clearly the ultimate goal—that lighthouse beacon I wrote about earlier—by which we should steer. As Yogi Berra said, "If you don't know where you're going, you'll end up somewhere else." So, keep your goals in mind. With your mind's eye, see yourself as being slim and healthy, confident and relaxed as you enjoy healthful, tasty, low-fat meals that satisfy and please you. Without Chitosan, this might be an unrealistic goal, a fantasy bound to lead to disappointment. But with this product, your dream can be simple reality. You can now afford to walk, talk, act, think, feel, and behave as if you were already successful at losing that undesired weight. You can act on the assumption that you will soon be slim and need never be fat again. And the reason you can act with such assurance is that with Chitosan it is true. Slowly and steadily, you will lose weight—and keep it off.

You now have the everyday tools for success. Move in the direction of the dietary plans I've laid out. If you don't get all the way there, don't worry about it. You'll still lose weight, only more slowly. But you have a long life ahead of you, so whether you lose weight a little faster or slower is really not that important. (You'll probably live longer now anyhow, so you'll still have the time to enjoy your slimmed down body.)

To the extent that you (like most of us) cannot stick to the ideal diet, use Chitosan to compensate. And use some extra to help you with occasional splurges. In other words, live an ordinary, sensible life, enjoy your food, balance it as well as you can, eat less than you did before, and keep doing it indefinitely because it is easy and practical to do so. Gradually, but inexorably, your weight will drop to safe and healthy levels. More important, your overall health will improve as you absorb less fat, thus reducing your risk of suffering from the killer diseases such as heart and brain attacks, cancer and diabetes, gallstones, arthritis problems associated with obesity, and other ailments.

Don't forget to exercise regularly. Once you get into the habit and see how great you feel, you'll *want* to exercise. Don't push too hard; the desire will grow organically, in spite of itself. In fact, as long as you do more exercise than before, you will be all right. Pushing yourself beyond your comfort zone will prove counterproductive. You want to *keep* exercising. You won't be able to do that unless you enjoy it. Eventually, exercise will become an important part of your life, not just an adjunct. For it really is important: It can save your life.

Be sure to talk to your doctor about the antioxidants and

other supplements discussed in this book. I have described a minimum amount that I believe is necessary to promote optimal health, to slow the aging process, to reduce the risk of cardiovascular disease, cancer, and other problems, and to keep the immune system strong. Your needs may vary, so talk to your nutritionally oriented physician soon.

Remember, always keep your larger goal in sight. It is excellent physical health and a body that is naturally well-proportioned, energetic, and smoothly functional. If you are seriously overweight now—and especially if you have been for quite a while—this may seem farfetched indeed. But don't worry. As Shakespeare said, "Assume the virtue, if you have it not." Approach the program with enthusiasm. How can you not feel enthusiastic about a program that, perhaps for the first time in your life, offers you an easier, realistic way to eliminate that excess fat without surgery, without dangerous drugs, and without a diet plan so intense you know going in it won't work for very long. But if you're enthusiastic now, just imagine how enthusiastic you'll be as you find yourself losing weight and gaining health . . . as you realize that *Chitosan really does work as I've assured you it will.*

Notes

1. Why Can't I Lose Weight?

1. Kuczmarski, R. J., et al. "Increasing Prevalence of Overweight Among U.S. Adults: The National Health and Nutrition Examination Survey, 1960 to 1991." *Journal of the American Medical Association* 1994; 272 (3): 205–11.

2. What's Wrong with Excess Weight?

1. Schatzkin, A., et al. "The Dietary Fat-Breast Cancer Hypothesis Is Alive." *Journal of the American Medical Association* 261 (22): 3284–87, 1989.

2. Howe, G., et al. "Dietary Factors and Risk of Breast Cancer: Combined Analysis of 12 Case-Controlled Studies." *Journal of the National Cancer Institute* 82:561–9, 1990.

3. Carroll, K. K. "Dietary Fat and Cancer." *American Journal of Clinical Nutrition* 53:1064S–7S, 1991.

4. Willett, W. C., et al. "Relation of Meat, Fat, and Fiber Intake to the Risk of Colon Cancer in a Prospective Study Among Women." *New England Journal of Medicine* 323:1664–72, 1990.

5. Whittemore, A., et al. "Diet, Physical Activity, and Colorectal Cancer Among Chinese in North America and China." *Journal of the National Cancer Institute* 82:915–26, 1990.

6. Calvert, R. J., et al. *Journal of the National Cancer Institute* 79 (4): 875, 1987.

7. "Nonpharmacological Approaches to the Control of High Blood Pressure." Final report of the Subcommittee on Nonpharmacological Therapy of the 1984 Joint National Committee on Detection, Evaluation, and Treatment of High Blood Pressure. *Hypertension* 8 (5): 444–467, 1986.

8. Chandra, R. K. "Nutrition and Immunity—Basic Considerations. Part 1." *Contemporary Nutrition* 11 (11), 1986. Levy, J. A. "Nutrition and the Immune System," in D. P. Stites, et al., eds. *Basic and Clinical Immunology.* Fourth ed. Los Altos, California: Lange Medical Publications, 1982: 297–305.

9. Palmblad, J. "Lymphocytes and Dietary Fat." *Lancet* 1997; 1:142.

10. Barone, J., et al. "Dietary Fat and Natural-Killer Cell Activity." *American Journal of Clinical Nutrition* 50: 861–67, 1989.

11. See, for example, Traut, E. E., Thrift, C. B. "Obesity in Arthritis: Related Factors, Dietary Factors." *Journal of the American Geriatric Society* 17: 710–717, 1969. See also Felson, D. T., et al. "Weight Loss Reduces the Risk for Symptom-

atic Knee Osteoarthritis in Women: The Framingham Study." *Annals of Internal Medicine* 116: 535–539, 1992.

12. National Institutes of Health Consensus Development Conference, December 8–10, 1986.

13. Anderson, J. "Update of HCF Diet Results." *HCF Newsletter* #4, June 1982, Lexington, Kentucky.

3. The Miracle of Chitosan

1. See, for example, Nauss, J. L., Thompson, J. L., Nagyvary, J. "The Binding of Micellar Lipids to Chitosan." *Lipids* 18 (10). L983, 714–719. Kanauchi, C., et al. "Mechanisms for the Fat Digestion by Chitosan. *Biosci Biotechnol Biochem* 1995, May, 59(5): 786–90. Deuchi, K., et al. "Decreasing Effect of Chitosan on the Apparent Fat Digestibility by Rats Fed on a High-Fat Diet." *Biosci Biotech Biochem* 1994; 58, 1613–6.

2. Nauss, J. L., Thompson, J. L., Nagyvary, J. "The Binding of Micellar Lipids to Chitosan." *Lipids* 18 (10). L983, 714–719.

3. Deuchi, K., et al. "Decreasing Effect of Chitosan on the Apparent Fat Digestibility by Rats Fed on a High-Fat Diet." *Biosci Biotech Biochem* 1994: 58, 1613–6.

4. Ibid.

5. Ibid.

6. Abelin, J., Lassus, A. "Fat Binder as a Weight-Reducer in Patients with Moderate Obesity." *ARM Medicina*, Helsinki, 1994, Aug.–Oct.

7. McDowell, M. A., et al. "Energy and Macronutrient Intakes of Persons Ages 2 Months and Over in the United States." Third International Health and Nutrition Examination Survey, Phase I: 1988–1991. Advance data from Vital & Health Statistics of the Centers for Disease Control and Prevention; No. 255. Hyattsville, Maryland: National Center for Health Statistics, 1994.

8. Birkervedt, G. S. "Clinical Report." Dovre Medical Centre, Fjellhammer, Norway, May 1991.

9. Ikeda, I., et al. "Interrelated Effects of Dietary Fiber and Fat on Lymphatic Cholesterol and Triglyceride Absorption in Rats." *Journal of Nutrition* 119:1383–1387, 1989.

10. Sharma, C. P., et al. "Lipoprotein Absorption onto Modified Chitosan Beads; Preliminary Study." *Biomater Artif Cells Immobilization Biotechnol.* 1993. 21: 659–664.

11. Kimie, A., et al. "Toxicity of Chitosan." In: *Clinical Compendium Volume 1: A Compilation of Current Scientific Information Relative to Chitosan*. Clovis, California: Intelligent Health, 1996.

5. Putting the Fat Blocker Program into Practice, and Why

1. See, for example, DeFronzo, R.A., Ferrannini E. "Insulin Resistance. A Multifaceted Syndrome Responsible for NIDDM, Obesity, Hypertension, Dyslipidemia, and Atherosclerotic Cardiovascular Disease." *Diabetes Care* 14 (3): 173–94, 1991. McNamara, D. J. "The Diet-Heart Question: How Good Is the Evidence?" *Contemp Nutr* 12 (4), 1987.

2. Blankenhorn, D. H., et al. "The Influence of Diet on the Appearance of New Lesions in Human Coronary Arteries." *Journal of the American Medical Association* 263 (12): 1646–52, 1990.

3. See, for example: Acheson, R. M., Williams, D. R. "Does Consumption of Fruit and Vegetables Protect Against Stroke?" *Lancet* 1: 1191–93, 1983.

4. Khaw, K. T., Barrett-Connor, E. "Dietary Potassium and Stroke-Associated Mortality: A 12-Year Prospective Population Study." *New England Journal of Medicine* 316 (5): 235–40, 1987.

5. Kearney, R. "Promotion and Prevention of Tumour Growth: Effects of Endotoxin, Inflammation and Dietary Lipids." *Int Clin Nutr Rev* 7 (4):157–68, 1987.

6. Steinbeck, G., et al. "Vitamin A, Supplements, Fried Foods, Fat and Urothelial Cancer. A Case-Referent Study in Stockholm in 1985–87." *Int J Cancer* 45:1006–11, 1990.

7. Zhao, L. P., et al. "Effects of Saturated Fat on Lung, Prostate, and Breast Cancer in Five Ethnic Groups of Hawaii." Abstract. *Am J Clin Nutr* 53: P–31, 1991.

8. Snowdon, D. A. Letter. *Journal of the American Medical Association* 254 (3): 356–7, 1985.

9. Rose, D. P. "Dietary Fiber and Breast Cancer." *Nutr Cancer* 13: 1–8, 1990. Hughes, R. E. "Hypothesis: A New Look at Dietary Fiber." *Hum Nutr Clin Nutr* 40C: 81–86, 1986.

10. Alberts, D., et al. "Effects of Dietary Wheat Bran Fiber on Rectal Epithelial Cell Proliferation in Patients with Resection for Colorectal Cancers." *J Natl Cancer Inst* 82: 1280–5, 1990. Greenward, P., Lanza, E. "Dietary Fiber and Colon Cancer." *Contemp Nutr* 11 (1), 1986. DeCossee, J. J., et al. "Effect of Wheat Fiber and Vitamins C and E on Rectal Polyps in Patients with Familiar Adenomatous Polyposis." *J Natl Cancer Inst* 81 (17): 1290–97, 1989.

11. Howe, G., et al. "Dietary Factors and Risk of Pancreatic Cancer: Results of a Canadian Population-Based Case-Control Study." *Int J Cancer* 45:604–08, 1990.

12. Ross, J., et al. "Dietary and Hormonal Evaluation of Men at Different Risks for Prostate Cancer: Fiber Intake, Excretion, and Composition, with In Vitro Evidence for an Association Between Steroid Hormones and Specific Fiber Components." *Am J Clin Nutr* 51: 365–70, 1990.

13. Steiner, G. Editorial: "From an Excess of Fat, Diabetics Die." *Journal of the American Medical Association* 262 (3): 398–99, 1989.

14. Nagy, K., et al. "High-Fat Feeding Induces Tissue-Specific Alteration in Proportion of Activated Insulin Receptors in Rats." *Acta Endocrinol* (Coph) 122 (3): 361–68, 1990. Warner, T., et al. "Alternation of Insulin-Receptor Kinase Activity by High-Fat Feeding." *Diabetes* 37 (10):1397–404, 1988.

15. Salmeron, J., et al. "Dietary Fiber, Glycemic Load, and Risk of Non-Insulin-Dependent Diabetes Mellitus in Women." *Journal of the American Medical Association* 1997, 277: 472–477.

16. National Institutes of Health Consensus Development Conference, December 8–10, 1986.

17. Trowell, H. C. "Dietary-Fiber Hypothesis of the Etiology of Diabetes Mellitus." *Diabetes* 24 (8): 762–65, 1975.

18. Jenkins, D. J., et al. "Starchy Foods and Fiber: Reduced Rate of Digestion and Improved Carbohydrate Metabolism." *Scand J Gastroenterol Suppl* 129: 132–41, 1987.

19. Anderson, J. W. "Recent Advances in Carbohydrate Nutrition and Metabolism in Diabetes Mellitus." *J Am Coll Nutr* 8 (Suppl): 61S–67S, 1989.

20. Koliado, V. B. "Effects of Unbalanced Diet in the Etiology and Course of Cholecystitis." *Vopr Pitan* (6): 23–27, 1983.

21. See, for example, Thornton, J. R., et al. "Diet and Gallstones: Effects of Refined Carbohydrates on Bile Cholesterol Saturation and Bile Acid Metabolism." *Gut* 24: 2–6, 1983.

22. Fellstrom, B., et al. "Dietary History and Dietary Records in Renal Stone Patients and Control." *Urol Res* 12:58, 1984. Griffith, H. M., et al. "A Control Study of Dietary Factors in Renal Stone Formation." *Br J Urol* 53: 416–20, 1981.

23. See, for example, Griffith, H. M., 1981, op. cit., and Smith, J. H., et al. "Nutrition and Urolithiasis." *New England Journal of Medicine* 298: 87–89, 1978.

24. Anderson, J. W., Tietyen-Clark, J. "Dietary Fiber: Hyperlipidemia, Hypertension, and Coronary Heart Disease." *Am J Gastroenterol* 81(10): 907–19, 1986.

25. Wright, A., et al. "Dietary Fibre and Blood Pressure." *British Medical Journal* 2: 1541–43, 1979.

26. Schlamowitz, P., et al. "Treatment of Mild to Moderate Hypertension with Dietary Fibre." Letter. *Lancet* 2: 622–23, 1987.

27. Jacobsson, I., et al. "Correlation of Fatty Acid Composition of Adipose Tissue Lipids and Serum Phosphatidycholine and Serum Concentrations of Micronutrients with Disease Duration in Rheumatoid Arthritis." *Ann Rheum Dis* 49: 901–5, 1990.

28. Kearney, J., et al. "Dietary Intakes and Adipose Tissue Levels of Linoleic Acid in Peptic Ulcer Disease." *British Journal of Nutrition* 62: 699–706, 1989.

29. Rydning, A., et al. "Prophylactic Effect of Dietary Fiber in Duodenal Ulcer Disease." *Lancet* 2: 736–39, 1982.

30. Malhotra, S. L. "A Comparison of Unrefined Wheat and Rice Diets in Management of Duodenal Ulcer." *Postgrad Med J* 54: 6–9, 1978.

7. Supplements and Eating Tips

1. See Clark, L., et al. "Effects of Selenium Supplementation for Cancer Prevention in Patients with Cancer of the Skin." *Journal of the American Medical Association* 1996; 276: 1957–1963.

11. Dieters Beware

1. Atkins, Robert. *Dr. Atkins' Diet Revolution*. New York: Bantam Books, 1972.

2. Landis, Robyn. *Bodyfueling*. New York: Warner Books, 1994.

3. Danbrot, Margaret. *The New Cabbage Soup Diet*. New York: St. Martin's Press, 1997.

4. D'Adamu, Peter, and Catherine Whitney. *Eat Right for Your Type*. New York: G. P. Putnam's Sons, 1996.

5. Diamond, Harvey and Marilyn, *Fit for Life*. New York: Warner Books, 1985.

6. Ibid., pp. 18–19.

7. Miller, Peter. *The New Hilton Head Metabolism Diet*. New York: Warner Books, 1996.

8. McDougall, John. *The McDougall Program For Maximum Weight Loss*. New York: Plume, 1994.

9. Katahn, Martin. *The Rotation Diet*. New York: Bantam Books, 1986.

10. Hirsch, Alan. *Dr. Hirsch's Guide to Sensational Weight Loss*. Rockport, Massachusetts: Element Books, 1997.

11. Callahan, Roger, with Paul Perry. *Why Do I Eat When I'm Not Hungry?* New York: Avon Books, 1991.

12. Sears, Barry, with Bill Lawren. *The Zone*. New York: Regan Books, 1995.

13. Berkeley, California: Ten Speed Press, 1984.

14. Bo-Linn, G. W., et al. "Starch Blockers—Their Effect on Calorie Absorption from a High-Starch Meal." *New England Journal of Medicine*. 307: 1413–16, 1982.